高校英语选修课系列教材

A COURSEBOOK OF SPOKEN
ENGLISH
FOR APPLIED COLLEGES

应用型大学英语
交际口语教程

主　编　高朝阳　钟雪文
副主编　张晓红　梁玉兰　杨　梅　常　伟
编　者〔排名不分先后〕　王海涛　田孟鑫　田　野
　　　　李雨虹　李　翔　吴星辰　佘志国　张宜华
　　　　张　健　陈江宏　罗　亮　原俊宁　彭新悦

U0331440

清華大学出版社
北京

内 容 简 介

本教材以应用型本科院校的人才培养为目标，充分考虑应用型本科院校学生的实际英语口语水平和学习需求，在编写时融入地方文化特色，让学生感到有话可说。全书共6个单元，话题涉及大学生活、我的家乡、特色美食、休闲旅行、购物、运动康养；单元内设计了丰富有趣的口语活动，并配有彩色图片，引导学生"看图说话"；教材中的音视频均由学生录制，容易激发学生口语练习的积极性；随文附带二维码，学习者可直接扫码听看。本教材可作为应用型本科院校大学英语基础课、选修课教材，也可作为口语练习材料，供学生自学使用。

版权所有，侵权必究。 举报：010-62782989，beiqinquan@tup.tsinghua.edu.cn。

图书在版编目（CIP）数据

应用型大学英语交际口语教程 / 高朝阳，钟雪文主编.—北京：清华大学出版社，2019(2023.8重印)
（高校英语选修课系列教材）
ISBN 978-7-302-53330-6

Ⅰ.①应… Ⅱ.①高…②钟 Ⅲ.①英语–口语–高等学校–教材 Ⅳ.①H319.32

中国版本图书馆CIP数据核字（2019）第161026号

责任编辑：黄智佳 刘 艳
封面设计：陈国熙
责任校对：王凤芝
责任印制：宋 林
出版发行：清华大学出版社
    网 址：http://www.tup.com.cn，http://www.wqbook.com
    地 址：北京清华大学学研大厦A座 邮 编：100084
    社 总 机：010-83470000 邮 购：010-62786544
    投稿与读者服务：010-62776969，c-service@tup.tsinghua.edu.cn
    质量反馈：010-62772015，zhiliang@tup.tsinghua.edu.cn
印 装 者：北京嘉实印刷有限公司
经 销：全国新华书店
开 本：185mm×260mm 印 张：7.75 字 数：140千字
版 次：2019年9月第1版   印 次：2023年8月第4次印刷
定 价：49.90元

产品编号：083642-01

前言
Preface

　　培养应用型人才是我国经济社会发展对高等教育提出的新要求，也是地方应用型本科高校的历史使命。应用型人才要求在一定的理论规范指导下，从事非学术研究性工作，具体到大学英语这门课程上就是培养学生的英语实际应用能力，培养学生用英语交流和解决问题的能力。英语交流能力分为口头交流能力和书面交流能力，对大多数学生来说，提高英语口头交流能力是最紧迫的任务。

　　针对这一实际需求，我们编写了这本《应用型大学英语交际口语教程》。本教材有以下特点：

　　针对校本人才培养：本教材专门针对应用型普通本科高校学生而编写，编写过程中充分考虑到应用型本科高校的人才培养目标和学生的实际英语水平。学生实际英语水平是英语口语教材编写的最主要依据。应用型本科院校学生的入学英语水平普遍较低，英语语音基础掌握得不牢固，相当部分的学生通过大学阶段的英语学习仍不能达到大学英语四级水平。因此，在教材编写过程中，我们不好高骛远，而是以学生实际英语水平和学习需要为准则进行编写。

　　融入地方文化特色：本教材编写过程中充分考虑到编者所在学校的地方文化特色和学校特色。人们只有在谈论自己熟悉的事情时才有话可说，因此在编写过程中，我们尽可能选择能够体现地方文化特色的素材，让学生感到有话可说。教材中专门加入了饮食文化、民俗文化等内容，这些内容都是学生所熟悉的，更能激发他们参与讨论的兴趣和积极性。

话题人文色彩浓厚：本教材共 6 个单元，话题涉及大学生活、我的家乡、特色美食、休闲旅行、购物、运动康养，与学生生活息息相关，富于人文关怀。

口语活动丰富有趣：单元内设计了丰富有趣的口语活动，并配有彩色图片，引导学生"看图说话"。教材中的音视频*均由学生录制，容易激发学生口语练习的积极性。随文附带二维码，学习者可直接扫码听看。

本教材可作为应用型本科院校大学英语基础课、选修课教材，也可作为口语练习材料，供学生自学使用。

教材中的部分图片来源于网络，因著作者不明无法取得联系，请相关图片著作者看到后及时与出版社或编者联系，以便支付稿酬。

由于编者水平有限，书中难免有不足之处，恳请读者批评指正。

编者

2019 年 2 月

---

* 本教材的音视频脚本，可从清华大学出版社资源库里免费下载，下载地址：ftp://ftp.tup.tsinghua.edu.cn/。

目录
Contents

Unit 1
College Life

Objectives

1. To know useful information about college life
2. To practice dialogues about college life
3. To describe pictures about college
4. To discuss topics about college

Warm-up Questions

1. Where are you studying now? What do you think about your college life?

2. What do you think you can benefit from your university?

3. Talk about a favorite class that you take in college. Why is it your favorite and what do you think you have learned from it?

Section A   Getting Ready to Speak

Part One   Reading for Information

Read the following passages and get useful information about college life.

Tips for Adjusting to University Life

For many first-year students, university may be their first experience living away from home for an extended period of time. It is a definite break from home. Here are some tips for students to adjust to university life.

The first few weeks on campus can be a lonely period. New relationships should not be expected to develop overnight. Living with roommates can present special, sometimes intense, problems. Negotiating respect of personal property, personal space, sleeping habit, and relaxation needs can be a complex task. The complexity increases if roommates are from different ethnic and cultural backgrounds with different values. Communicating one's legitimate needs calmly, listening with respect to a roommate's concerns, and being willing to compromise to meet each other's most important needs can promote resolution of issues.

Roommates may work out mutually satisfying living arrangements, but the reality is that each one may tend to have his or her own circle of friends.

University courses are a great deal more difficult than high school courses. In order to survive, a student must take responsibility for his or her actions. This means he/she needs to follow the course outlines and keep up with the courses.

How to Choose a College Major

Selecting a college major is a personal decision and you have to spend time reflecting on your goals, likes, dislikes, skills, and so on. Here are some tips:

Ask questions

Some factors to consider when selecting a college major:

What are your interests?

Which subjects did you enjoy studying the most in high school?

What skills do you have?

Do you have any hobby that you would like to pursue as a career?

What have you learned about your like and dislike from your experience?

The answers to these questions can help guide your selection of a college major. For example, if you held a part-time job in retail while in high school and you absolutely hated the work, you can immediately scratch retail management off your list. However, if you enjoyed the part of the job that involved setting up product displays, you might seriously want to consider a major in visual merchandising.

Don't be panic

Selecting a college major is an important decision, and it is not one that should be made lightly. It is important to remember, however, that declaring a major is not an irreversible decision. It is not uncommon for college students to change majors one or more times after enrolling in college. Set college goals, do your researches, keep an open mind, and be honest with yourself, and you can choose a college major that will steer you down the path to success.

College Social Life

In college, maintaining your social life and expanding your social circle are very important and should not be neglected. Not only is socializing beneficial for your health, happiness, and your self-confidence, but it's also a great way to learn outside of the classroom. Here's why college social life is important.

Make study easier

It makes study easier if someone is there to help you. Study partners can not only teach you new study techniques, but can also help you study more efficiently and keep you on track.

Expose to different cultures

Exposing yourself to a variety of social situations, whether it be joining a club, going to a party, or eating dinner downtown with your friends, allows you to develop relationships with people from different places and cultures. Expanding your social circle will help you form cross-cultural connections as well as develop a greater world perspective. Interacting with people from different backgrounds will teach you more about life than any college course will.

Keep you emotionally stable

Humans are inherently social beings. We need to interact with people in order to maintain our sense of self and stay sane. Have you ever noticed how much better and less stressed you feel after talking to a friend about a horrible day? Then maybe you should make that a routine. Do not neglect your emotions. Taking time for yourself is just as important as taking time for your courses.

Build your self-confidence

Surrounding yourself with people who like you will help boost your self-esteem and encourage personal growth. During college you may be placed in social situations that can be out of your comfort zone and make you feel vulnerable, but if you push yourself to interact with others, you can develop your social skills and build your self-confidence.

Impact your future

The social life you choose to have in college can greatly affect your future endeavors. The friends you make in college may become co-workers and allies in the work force. You have already started building your professional network, so keep it up!

Part Two　Dialogue Samples

Practice the following dialogues with your partner. Change the role when necessary.

Ann: Morning, Jennifer. You look rather pretty on this pink dress.

Jennifer: Thank you. Yesterday was my birthday and mom gave it to me as a gift.

Ann: Though maybe it is a bit late, but still "Happy Birthday".

Jennifer: Thank you anyway. By the way, how do you handle the course selection? Ah! I'm still confused about it and can not decide which to take.

Ann: I have been planning since last term but still not decided. On one hand, there are so many courses which are practical for later career. On the other hand, several distinguished professors will give lectures this term. However, our time and energy are limited, so it is really hard to make a final decision.

Jennifer: Yeah. We cannot have our cake and eat it. What you said just now reminds me that I have to take future career into consideration as well. I have never thought of that before. Then why not take two practical classes and two lectures given by our famous professors?

Ann: Sounds good. As for me, I think I will take Chinese and applied mathematics as the practical classes and at the same time follow the lectures in anthropology and cognitive science given by our famous professors.

Jennifer: Chinese? I was considering taking this course, too. But those who had taken it said it is rather hard for us whose native language is of the Indo-European language family.

Ann: Anyway, I'm charmed by the Chinese language and culture and I think speaking Chinese will bring much convenience when we hunt for a job. So I would like to take the challenge.

Jennifer: Uh, I think it deserves your hard work. And I want to have a try, too. Then when we can speak some Chinese, we can travel to China together.

Ann: Good idea. Profound history and beautiful scenery in China are so attractive. Then, what about you? What's your decision?

Jennifer: Besides Chinese, I would like to take African studies, economics and literature. You know that Africa is undeveloped and there are so many poor people who need urgent help. When I have a basic knowledge of Africa, I can explain to the public and call on them to do something within their power.

Ann: You are so kind-hearted. And I think after class you can surf the Internet to find more information and pictures about Africa if you like. Still there are three courses which I have a great passion for. It's a pity that I have to give them up.

Jennifer: Don't worry! Maybe you can borrow the suggested readings and notes from our classmates who choose these classes and read them by yourself. And when you have trouble in understanding, you can ask them for help.

Ann: Good idea. By doing so, twice can be accomplished with half the effort. You are such a smart girl. Thank you very much.

Jennifer: Not at all. I'm sorry I must leave now. I have an appointment at 10 a.m. See you next time.

Ann: See you.

Kevin: How are you doing, Ann?

Ann: Fine. And you? How about your college life?

Kevin: Great! I study in Arts and Sciences College of Sichuan Normal University.

Ann: Yes, I've heard that it was founded in 1999 and is one of the independent institutes of our province.

Kevin: That's right. Its two campuses are located respectively in Chengdu and Jingtang County.

Ann: How many hectares does it cover?

Kevin: It covers an area of more than 66.7 hectares.

Ann: Wow, great! Your campus must be very beautiful.

Kevin: Em, it has a good environment for study.

Ann: Any more information about your college?

Kevin: Over the past 10 years, guided by the college motto: Arts for Virtue, Sciences for Truth, Unity in Diversity, Progress in Development, it has accumulated rich experience in offering educational programs.

Ann: Now, how many students are there in your college?

Kevin: It has a total enrollment of about 18,000 full-time students.

Ann: How about teachers?

Kevin: Our college has a high-level team of faculty including 800 full-time teachers.

Ann: Huge number!

Kevin: Our college has set up 2 research institutions and 14 departments. The library has plenty of books in its collection and has access to many E-books of diverse contents.

Ann: How many specialties does your college offer?

Kevin: It offers more than 60 specialties to undergraduates.

Ann: Great! If there is a chance, I want to visit your college.

Kevin: Welcome to our college. I can be your guide.

Ann: Oh, thank you!

Robert: Have you been to our campus BBS recently? There is a hot issue that attracts me. People are arguing whether it is good for us to take part in social activities. What's your opinion?

John: In my opinion, it is positive to attend social activities in college. Students can benefit a lot and it would be very helpful for their future careers.

Robert: Can you explain in detail?

John: Definitely. Through attending these social activities, students can meet a lot of people and enlarge their social circles, and they can improve their abilities to deal with interpersonal relationships.

Robert: It does make sense. But I think it would waste a lot of time if students attend these social activities and it would distract students' attention from their studies.

John: I'm not in agreement with what you say. Mastering all the knowledge in the textbooks is not the only prerequisite for getting a good job. I know some graduates who are excellent in their studies, but know little about interpersonal communication, which has been an obstacle in their future work and lives.

Robert: However, for some students, these social activities are far more attractive than the classes. They take part in them just for fun . And finally they would neglect their studies and be misled and go astray.

John: That's possible. But in my eyes, a successful university education is to cultivate talents not only mastering all the knowledge and skills in the textbooks but also having abilities to handle interpersonal relationships. It's true that some of the students are not mature enough to distinguish the true from the false. But these students can get useful experience by participating in social activities, and they can have healthy and all-round development.

Robert: I still can't agree with you. Social activities would take students' minds off their studies, which would have a negative effect on their studies.

John: From the beginning to the end, I believe that learning to deal with human interaction is a part of university education and students can develop these skills by taking part in various social

activities. Therefore, social activities have positive effects on university studies.

Robert: Maybe you are right, but let's agree to disagree.

Part Three   Useful Expressions

Expressions below may help you talk about campus life.

- a good social reputation 良好的社会声誉
- a sound learning atmosphere 良好的学习氛围
- academic activity 学术活动
- adult higher education 成人高等教育
- advanced talents with practical skills 高素质应用型人才
- comprehensive university 综合性大学
- compulsory/optional course 必修/选修课
- curriculum 课程
- college entrance examination 高考
- Department of Biology 生物系
- Department of Foreign Languages 外语系
- Department of Art 美术系
- Department of Chemistry 化学系
- Department of Chinese Language and Literature 中文系
- Department of Education 教育系
- Department of Math and Information Technology 数学与信息技术系
- Department of Physical Education 体育系
- Department of Physics and Electronic Engineering 物理电子工程系
- Department of Politics and Law 政法系
- Department of Tourism Management 旅游管理系
- discipline 学科
- educational background 教育背景

- educational highlights 课程重点部分
- educational history 学历
- foreign student 留学生
- freshman 大学一年级学生
- grant-in-aid system 助学金制度
- higher vocational education 高等职业教育
- intern 实习生
- junior 大学三年级学生
- liberal art 文科
- major 主修
- minor 副修
- physical activity 体育活动
- political and ideological education 政治思想教育
- post doctorate 博士后
- recreational activity 娱乐活动
- senior 大学四年级学生
- social activity 社会活动
- social practice 社会实践
- sophomore 大学二年级学生
- to become educated through independent study 自学成才
- to call the roll 点名
- to earn a credit 修学分
- to have both integrity and ability 德才兼备
- to register for/sign up for/enroll in/enlist in/take 选（课或专业）
- to shift/transfer to 转（系或专业）
- to waive a course 免修一门课程
- undergraduate 大学本科生

- What's your major?
  你学什么专业的?

- My major is.../I major in...
  我的专业是……

- What are your minor subjects?
  你辅修什么课程?

- I minor in...
  我辅修……

- What do you want to do after graduating from university?
  你毕业后打算做什么工作呢?

- My job is not in line with my major.
  我的工作和专业不对口。

- Nowadays, our abilities and skills are more important than the name of the university.
  现今，我们的能力与技能比学校的名声更重要。

- However, due to unsatisfied grades, I was rejected by my first-choice university.
  然而，由于分数不够，我没有被第一志愿学校录取。

- My roommates are all very friendly and sincere. We like to communicate and study together.
  我的室友都特别友好、真诚。我们喜欢在一起交流、学习。

- Now we have a lot of courses, and most are difficult, it takes us more time to learn. The teachers are rich in teaching experience and have a sense of responsibility. They give lectures meticulously and carefully.

目前我们的课程很多，而且大部分都比较难，需要花费更长的时间来学习。老师们有丰富的教学经验，有责任感，讲课细致认真。

- Our university is located in the downtown of Panzhihua City, well known as the Capital of Vanadium and Titanium in China, and the biggest base of iron and steel industry in western China. The city lies in the southwest of Sichuan Province and borders northwestern Yunnan Province.

我们学校坐落于攀枝花市中心。攀枝花被誉为"中国钒钛之都"，是我国西部最大的钢铁工业基地，位于四川省西南部，与云南省西北部接壤。

- Presently there are over 1,000 faculty members in our university. The university now has a total enrollment of over 12,000 students including full-time undergraduate, college and adult students.

目前我校的教职员工超过 1 000 人。在校学生超过 12 000 人，包括全日制普通本专科学生和成人教育学生。

- There are 12 schools and departments providing undergraduate courses in 52 specialties in our university. The 12 schools and departments are: School of Intelligent Manufacturing, School of Civil and Architectural Engineering, School of Mathematics and Computer Science, School of Humanities and Social Science, School of Foreign Languages and Cultures, School of Economics and Management, Art School, School of Transportation and Automotive Engineering, College of Vanadium and Titanium, School of Biological and Chemical Engineering, Medical Science School, School of Health and Wellness.

我校共有 12 个院系，开设有 52 个本科专业。这 12 个院系为：智能制造学院、土木与建筑工程学院、数学与计算机学院、人文社科学院、外国语学院、经济与管理学院、艺术学院、交通与汽车工程学院、钒钛学院、生物与化学工程学院、医学院、康养学院。

- Currently, our university offers a wide range of programs covering nine branches of learning such as science, engineering, liberal arts, law, economics, management, arts, agronomy and medical science.

  目前，学校开设了涵盖理、工、文、法、经、管、艺、农、医等9个学科门类的专业课程。

- Our university has formed a multi-disciplinary education mode while focusing on engineering, covering general higher education, higher vocational education and adult higher education.

  我校现已形成以工为主，多学科协调发展的办学模式，涵盖普通高等教育、高等职业教育和成人高等教育。

- In the past 30 years since its founding, nearly 40,000 students have graduated from our university. They are popular because of their excellent comprehensive quality and have become the backbone in the local economic and social development.

  建校30多年来，学校已为社会培养近4万名毕业生。他们因具备较好的综合素质而广受好评，已成为地方经济和社会发展的骨干力量。

- Our university stresses the importance of domestic and international academic exchange and cooperation. It has established intercollegiate exchanges and cooperation with some institutions of higher education in the countries such as Italy, Canada, Australia, and Sweden, etc.

  我们学校一贯重视国内、国际的学术交流与合作，已经和意大利、加拿大、澳大利亚以及瑞典的一些高校建立了校际交流与合作联系。

- We benefit a lot from the grant-in-aid system established by the university to encourage and help students with financial problems to accomplish their studies.

  学校为鼓励和帮助经济困难的学生完成学业而建立了助学金制度，我们从中获益颇多。

Section B　Local Specialties

Look at the following pictures and get to know what they are about according to the describing words.

Jing Ming Lake, with beautiful view and quiet environment, located near the library, is a small manual lake inside the campus. It can be seen that some students reading English in the morning by the lake and some young lovers walking together hand by hand in the evening.

The indoor English corner is usually held in room 206 of Number 2 Teaching Building on Wednesday evenings when some voluntary English-major students come and chat with each other in English under the guidance of foreign teachers. Sometimes simple and funny games are played here, from which students can get lots of fun.

The newly built Number 3 Cafeteria is located behind the Number 12 Dormitory Building and near the teachers' family dormitory building. It serves delicious dishes and Sichuan specialties. Many teachers also come here and have lunch during work days.

During the annual sports meeting, various track and field events are held in the sports ground, including running races, high jump, long jump, javelin throwing and so on. One of the participants from School of Foreign Languages and Cultures is putting the shot.

5

The volleyball court is a lively and funny place in our university, where a lot of students come to play volleyball together in the evening. The volleyball match is held annually in April. Teachers and students can all join the game. One of the ace spikers from School of Foreign Languages and Cultures is smashing in the court.

6

September is the college freshman month, during which about 5,000 students come to our university for study. Some reception sites are built to welcome and help the freshmen to do the registration, where some senior volunteers and teachers are guiding the freshmen and their parents.

7

Morning reading and night self-study is a tradition in our university. In the morning, a lot of students come to read indoors or outdoors. Some English major students are reading English in the Zhiyuan Square in front of Number 1 Teaching Building.

8

The welcome party for the freshmen is usually held at or near the New Year's Day. Freshmen, sophomores and junior students join the party to show themselves by singing, dancing and so on. One of the English-major girls is dancing to the rhythm of mixed music with both the eastern and western elements.

Section C   Oral Practices

Part One   Describing Pictures

Look at the following pictures and talk with your partner using the prompting words.

 Track and Field Events

Prompting words: 1,500-meter running race; 200-meter running race; finishing line; cheer

02 Opening Ceremony of the Sports Meeting

Prompting words: playground; vitality; vigorous posture; enthusiasm

03 English Speaking Contest

Prompting words: FLTRP Cup; contestants; judges; first-prize winner; excellent winners

04 English Debate Competition

Prompting words: honorable judges; distinguished guests; final statement; debater; affirmative side; negative side

05 Basketball Match

Prompting words: rebound; leap; score; team cooperation; layup; slam dunk; steal

06 Activities of Students' Association

Prompting words: volunteer; Students' Union; welcome party for the freshmen; extracurricular activities

07 English Corner

Prompting words: practice spoken English; smiling face; foreign teacher; encouraging nod

08 Stadium of Panzhihua University

Prompting words: well-equipped facilities; football field; jogging; sports meeting

Part Two Group Discussion

Discuss the following topics with your partner.

1. **College life is very important in people's lives. You need to make serious decision when choosing your college and major.**

   So, what have you considered when choosing your university or major?

2. **It's never an easy decision for a student to change his/her major. The major doesn't completely define a person, but it does help to seize the best opportunities to live out his/her purpose in life. If you think you aren't on the right track, it's feasible to shake things up.**

   So, what do you think are reasons for changing majors? And if you are not satisfied with your major now or have the opportunity to change it, what would you do?

3. **Nowadays, campus love is popular, but people hold different opinions about it. People who are against campus love maintain that it wastes time and money. While others declare nothing is more wonderful than love. They say that university students are adults, and they can handle their own affairs well enough.**

   So, what do you think of campus love? Should college students have their campus love? State your opinion and explain why.

4. **In your life so far, you probably have had some unforgettable experiences, had some sweet memories, and overcome something tough.**

   Describe an unforgettable experience in your school life, such as an experience that changed something and somehow transformed your life.

5. **Many studies have shown that there is a positive relationship between sport and academic achievement. It's said that college students who visit their campus gyms frequently are more likely to succeed in the classroom. Talk about your opinions, and your talk may include:**

   Have you ever gone to the gym?

   What's your favorite sport? How often do you exercise?

   What's your opinion on the relationship between physical exercise and learning ability?

Section D   Extended Reading

Read the following passage that may help you better understand the topic of this unit.

The Effects of Seating Position in Lecture Halls on Grades

Choice of seating in the lecture hall can affect a college student's performance, a study suggests.

Researchers from Sheffield Hallam University in the UK examined students' reasons for choosing particular seats in a lecture hall, and investigated how seating positions correlate with student performance.

Many students preferred to sit with their friends, while others were more concerned with either attracting or avoiding the lecturer's attention. Some students chose seats that allowed them to see and hear clearly, while others picked easily vacatable seats that made them feel less anxious, researchers said. Friendship groups who sat together tended to achieve similar grades, and students who sat alone at the edges tended to do worse than average.

So, where do you like to sit in a lecture hall? In fact, the choice of seat can not only affect your academic performance, but also reflect your personality.

The front rows

Appraising classroom rows based on academic performance, some professors have observed that the front rows remain prime sitting position typically held by outgoing scholarly students. "I notice the more prepared and personable students sit in front rows," said Dr. Chris Hammons, interim Dean of the College of Arts and Humanities and Chair of the Department of Education

(London). "Students in the front almost always score higher on exams."

Perhaps more importantly, sitting closer to the front of the room does have an effect on student-teacher rapport, which is linked to greater academic performance. According to a study published in 2013, GPAs decreased by 0.1 point on a four-point scale for every row further back which students sit.

The middle rows

Still, some students prefer the middle rows. This location in the classroom can make paying attention difficult depending on the student. In fact, Dr. Robert Wallace, a member of the National Education Association, considers choosing to sit in the middle of the classroom is one of the worst decisions a student can make. "In a classroom setting, a speaker's eyes tend to go to the front of the room and the back," he wrote in an article for Creators.com. "They don't look at the center of a room as often or with the same amount of attention."

The back rows

If neither the front nor middle is suitable for students, there can only be one other solution: the back.

For the broker on the value of classroom seating, the back row would have the lowest value. This fringe vicinity of the physical classroom often plays host to the biggest distractions. Many distractions occur at the back of the classroom. That's where students would chat, play video games and do some other stuff which the teacher must not know about. With the advent of Facebook and the likes, the situation would be worse by now.

教室座位的选择对成绩的影响

研究显示，教室座位的选择可能会影响大学生的学业成绩。

英国谢菲尔德哈勒姆大学的研究人员分析了学生们在课堂中选择特定座位的原因，并调查了他们所选择的座位和学业成绩之间的关系。

许多学生喜欢和朋友坐在一起，而另外一些学生则希望引起或避开授课老师的注意。有些学生选择那些能让他们清楚地看到和听到老师讲课的座位，而其他学生则偏爱那些让他们觉得不那么焦虑的座位，因为他们可以方便地起身离开教室。坐在一起的一群朋友倾向于获得相似的成绩，而独自坐在教室角落的学生的成绩往往低于平均水平。

那么，你最喜欢坐在教室的哪个位置呢？其实，座位的挑选不仅能影响你的学业成绩，还能反映你的个性特征。

前排

一些教授基于学业成绩对学生在教室中的座位进行评价，他们注意到，开朗活泼且博学的学生最爱坐前排。艺术与人文学院临时院长、伦敦教育部主席克里斯·哈蒙斯博士说："我注意到，准备越充分、越品学兼优的学生越爱坐在前排。坐在前排的学生通常考试成绩更好。"

或许更重要的是，坐在教室前排还能促进师生关系和谐，从而带来更好的学业成绩。根据 2013 年发表的一项研究，学生每靠后坐一排，GPA 成绩就下降 0.1 分（总分为 4 分）。

中间

有些学生选择坐在教室中间的座位，这种位置会使一些学生更难集中注意力。事实上，全美教育协会成员罗伯特·华莱士博士认为，中间排的座位是最差的选择之一。他在发表于创作者网站的一篇文章中说："在教室里，老师的目光总是落在前排或者后排。他们不怎么看中间排的学生，或者给予的关注没那么多。"

后排

如果前排和中间排都不合适，他们就只能坐在后排了。

如果要评估教室座位的价值，那么后排价值最低。后排是教室的边缘地带，学生最容易分心。教室后排的学生最容易走神。后排的学生常常聊天、玩电子游戏或者忙一些老师们肯定不知道的事儿。脸书等社交媒体出现后，这种情况肯定更糟糕了。

Unit 2
My Hometown

Objectives

1. To know useful information about places
2. To practice dialogues about hometown
3. To describe pictures of or about a place
4. To discuss topics about hometown

Warm-up Questions

1 Where is your hometown? Do you like it? Why?
2 What tourist attractions are there in your hometown?
3 Do you think your hometown is a good living place for young people? Why?

Section A   Getting Ready to Speak

Part One   Reading for Information

Read the following passages and get useful information about these places.

Panzhihua City

Panzhihua City is located at the junction of Sichuan Province and Yunnan Province in southwestern China. It lies in the upper reach of Yangtze River. The city's name "Panzhihua" comes from a kind of flower named kapok which is as red as flame and as bright as morning glow when it comes into full blossom in spring. It is the only city named after a flower in China and known for the saying "flower is the city and the city is flower". As for administrative divisions, Panzhihua City consists of East District, West District, Renhe District, Miyi County and Yanbian County under its jurisdiction with an area of 7,440 square kilometers and 1.23 million population. Its urbanization rate is approximately 65.34%, ranking the top second in Sichuan Province. And due to 98% urban citizens coming from different cities, the city is known as a migrant city.

Chongqing City

Chongqing is situated at the transitional area between the Tibetan Plateau and the Middle-Lower Yangtze Plain. It has a subtropical climate and is often swept by moist monsoons. It often rains at night in late spring and early summer, and thus the city is famous for its "night rain in the Ba Mountains", as described in ancient Chinese poems, for example the famous "Written on a Rainy Night—A Letter to the North" by Li Shangyin.

Chongqing is a major city in southwestern China. Administratively, it is one of China's four municipalities under direct administration of the central government (the other three are Beijing, Shanghai and Tianjin).

Chongqing has a population of over 30 million, spreading over an area the size of Austria.

Chengdu City

The city of Chengdu holds a significant position in economic, cultural and administrative history of ancient China. Situated in the southwestern part of China, this capital of Sichuan Province is widely renowned for its cultural heritage amid unparallel natural beauty.

About 2,000 years ago, Shu Dynasty established their capital in Chengdu. This thousand-year-old city has derived its unique name in the Chinese word for Land of Abundance (天府之国). Another name which denotes the city of Chengdu is Brocade City or Jin Cheng (锦城).

The wide area of the city which provides habitats to more than 10,000,000 people is more than 12,000 square kilometers. Located in the western border of Sichuan Basin, Chengdu is featured by the balmy and moist winter. Snow is not common in winter of Chengdu except certain amount of frost every year. Summer lasts for long and rain attains its zenith in this season. The climatic condition in spring is the most fascinating.

Part Two Dialogue Samples

Practice the following dialogues with your partner. Change the role when necessary.

Bill: Hello, nice to meet you! I'm Bill.

Amy: Nice to meet you, too! I'm Amy. I don't think I've seen you around before.

Bill: No. I just started working here this month, in the Sales Department.

Amy: Just now, I heard that you come from Wenzhou! That's a nice city, isn't it?

Bill: Yes, that's right! As a rich city in Zhejiang Province, Wenzhou is one of Zhejiang's economic centers as well as being one of the most important centers for international trade and communications.

Amy: Great! So, I think Wenzhou must be one of the highly developed cities in China! By the way, is there something tasty in your hometown?

Bill: Certainly, in my hometown, sweet food is the most acceptable. Besides, I like dumpling very much, especially dumpling with pork!

Amy: Ah ha! Sounds interesting. Could you please tell me something about Wenzhou cuisine?

Bill: Sure. Wenzhou cuisine is characterized by its elaborate preparation and various techniques of cooking, such as sauteing, stewing, and stir- and deep-frying.

Amy: That sounds special! I can't wait to try some Wenzhou food actually.

Bill: You can try many kinds of food there and it will be a great experience. Generally speaking, Wenzhou food tastes fresh and crisp, varying with the change of season. People always put much sugar when cooking.

Amy: You don't like spicy food, do you?

Bill: No, I don't. The more sweet, the more I love!

Amy: What's the weather like in Wenzhou then?

Bill: The weather in Wenzhou is so comfortable that it is really a nice city for people to stay long in China, I promise! Although the weather in summer is a little hot, but winter is so charming!

Amy: I really want to take a trip to Wenzhou! Call me next time if you go back to your hometown!

Bill: Ok. I am sure I will be the best guide in my hometown! Just believe me!

Amy: Can't wait for that.

Yangyun: Hello, nice to meet you! I'm Yangyun. I come from Leshan.

Linjing: Nice to meet you, too! I'm Linjing from Lijiang.

Yangyun: Lijiang? I know it. It's an ancient town in Yunnan Province.

Linjing: Yes. It's famous for natural scenery and colorful cultures. It also has been known as City of Love. Plenty of legends about people who live for love and die for love circulate among the local people. So, it is regarded as the paradise of love and romance. Just now, you said you come from Leshan! Wow, I have heard that Leshan is a very beautiful place.

Yangyun: Yeah! Leshan is a famous tourist attraction in China, and Leshan Giant Buddha is extremely well-received all around the world. At the foot of the Giant Buddha, we can feel how tiny we are! On the other hand, people in my hometown are very friendly and hospitable.

Linjing: Oh, I really want to go there! By the way, is there any local specialty?

Yangyun: In my hometown, Leshan Bobo chicken (钵钵鸡) is the most acceptable.

Linjing: Sounds tasty. What's that?

Yangyun: It's a dish with such a variety of ingredients as chicken, duck tongues, shrimps and vegetables. Being served in a Bo (big bowel), so it's called Bobo chicken. The dish tastes hot and spicy. It's really appetizing.

Linjing: Ah ha!!! I like it. In Lijiang, the favorite snack is Lijiang Baba (丽江粑粑). It's a kind of cake made by the local fine wheat, ham and oil. It has two kinds of taste, salty and sweet.

Yangyun: Oh, I really want to have a taste.

Linjing: Lijiang Baba can be kept for a few days. I may take it for you next time.

Yangyun: Great! Thank you!

Linjing: You're welcome.

John: So, Katie, you are from England, right?

Katie: Uh-hmm, that's right.

John: Are you from a big town?

Katie: No, I'm from a very small town.

John: Oh, what's its name?

Katie: It's in the southwest. It's called Torquay.

John: Torquay. Is it a fun place to live?

Katie: I think so. It's very famous in the UK, because we have lots of beautiful beaches.

John: Oh, that's nice. Can you recommend a restaurant in your town? Where is a good place to have dinner?

Katie: There are lots of amazing restaurants along the sea front. So, you can sit in a restaurant and look at the beach at the same time.

John: Oh, that's romantic!

Katie: Yes, it's really beautiful.

John: Is it expensive?

Katie: It depends on which restaurant you go to. If you go to an Italian restaurant, that's going to be expensive.

John: So, what kind of foods do they have?

Katie: They have all kinds of foods, but the most popular food in my hometown is Italian food and Chinese food.

John: No British food?

Katie: No.

John: That's interesting. Then, is there any good place to do exercises in your town?

Katie: Of course. We have lots of parks and people always play football in the parks.

John: That sounds great. People can get close to the nature!

Katie: Yes. And there are also so many beautiful beaches in Torquay, where you can enjoy the natural scenery of the sea.

John: Nice. Thank you for telling me.

Katie: You're welcome.

Part Three   Useful Expressions

Expressions below may help you talk about your hometown.

- ancient architectural complex 古建筑群
- chemical industry 化工业
- clothing industry 服装业
- countryside 农村，乡村
- densely-populated 人口稠密的
- fascinating fairyland 仙境；奇境
- heavy industry 重工业
- holiday resort 度假区；度假胜地
- human landscape 人文景观
- independent traveler 旅游散客
- industrialized 工业化的
- landscape/scenery with mountains and rivers 山水风光
- light industry 轻工业
- manufacturing 制造业
- medium-sized city 中型城市
- metropolis 大都市
- mineral bath 矿泉浴
- municipality 自治市或区；直辖市
- scenic spots and historical sites 名胜古迹
- sparely-populated 人口稀少的
- stockbreeding 畜牧业
- to feast one's eyes 让某人一饱眼福
- tourist attractions/scenic spots 旅游景点

- 百花竞放 hundreds of flowers contend to blossom
- 大众之城 the city of commoners
- 东方之珠 Pearl of the Orient
- 动感之都 a dynamic city
- 独具匠心 original design; unique pattern
- 湖光山色 landscape of lakes and hills
- 湖石假山 lakeside rocks and rockeries
- 景色如画 picturesque views
- 久负盛名 long established and prestigious
- 名山大川 famous mountains and great rivers
- 人间仙境 fairyland on earth
- 人在画中游 traveling in a pictorial world
- 山清水秀 beautiful mountains and clear waters
- 赏心悦目 a feast to the eye
- 食在广州 eating in Guangzhou
- 天堂之旅 a trip to the paradise; a journey to the heaven
- 味在成都 delicacies in Chengdu
- 依山傍水 enclosed/surrounded by hills on one side and waters on the other
- 诱人景色 inviting views
- 郁郁葱葱 lush green; luxuriant vegetation
- 远离尘嚣 a true departure; an escape from the bustling
- 卓越不俗 excellent but not fancy
- 醉在贵州 intoxicated in Guizhou

- I'm from…/I come from…
  我来自……

- I grew up in a small village surrounded by mountains.
  我在一个群山环抱的小山村长大。

- There are so many fond memories of my hometown.
  我对家乡有许多美好的回忆。

- When I was a boy, I enjoyed spring in my hometown because I could y kites.
  小时候,我喜欢家乡的春天,因为可以放风筝。

- My hometown is known for its local delicacies.
  我家乡的小吃很出名。

- It gives me great pleasure to introduce my hometown.
  很荣幸能向大家介绍我的家乡。

- People in my hometown are diligent and hardworking.
  我家乡的人们勤劳肯干。

- My hometown is richly endowed with natural resources.
  我的家乡资源丰富,得天独厚。

- I'm proud of my hometown for its beautiful scenery and long-standing history.
  我的家乡风景优美,历史悠久,我为她感到骄傲。

- My hometown is quite different from what it was ten years ago.
  我的家乡过去十年发生了很大的变化。

- Where is your hometown?
  你的家乡在哪里?

- Have you ever visited my hometown?
  你去过我的家乡吗?

- What's the weather like in your hometown?
  你家乡的天气怎么样?

- My hometown enjoys a reputation for its rich cultures.
  我的家乡因文化丰富而著名。

- Could you please tell me something about your hometown?
  你能给我讲讲你的家乡吗?

- What's the most unforgettable memory of your hometown?
  你对家乡最难忘的记忆是什么?

- What's the most famous scenic spot in your hometown?
  你家乡最著名的景点是什么?

- What's the most famous food in your hometown?
  你家乡最著名的美食是什么?

- What's the first impression a visitor would have on your hometown?
  游客对你家乡的第一印象会是怎样的?

- How often do you go back to your hometown?
  你多久回老家一次?

Section B   Local Specialties

Look at the following pictures and get to know what they are about according to the describing words.

Panzhihua is home to two river systems, Jinsha River and Yalong River, along which there are as many as 95 rivers in the city. It is known as the First City in the Upper Reaches of the Yangtze River. At present, within 30 kilometers of Jinsha River, there are eight highway bridges and within 20 kilometers of Yalong River, there are four. That's why Panzhihua is called the Bridge Museum.

Miyi County is subordinate to Panzhihua. The downtown of Miyi County is flat, which is quite rare in Panzhihua. Because of its beautiful view and ample sunlight, it becomes a relatively famous resort.

The road to the airport of Panzhihua is the favorite cycling road for young people. In addition to its nice road condition, people love the great view while riding on it.

Panzhihua is built by mountains and waters, the night vision of its downtown is tridimensional and impressive. It is fancy to look out to the downtown in the evening.

5

Panzhihua is named after kapok flower. This kind of flower is big and red just like a bunch of dancing flame. And interestingly, the flower is edible and delicious.

6

The Third-Front Construction Museum is located in Panzhihua, Sichuan Province. It is the largest, the most comprehensive and the most influential theme museum of the Third-Front Construction in China, which fully displays the historical features of the Third-Front Construction in 13 provinces and regions across the country. Now it has become the most attractive cultural card of Panzhihua.

7

Panzhihua is the only subtropical fruit-production base in Sichuan Province, abounding in mango, wax apple, pomegranate, sugar apple, cherry and so on. There are fresh fruits in all seasons. With wide varieties and superior quality, Panzhihua mango is the most popular among all fruits, which sells well at home and abroad. The mango in this picture is famous for its red color, and it has a smell of flower when you eat it.

8

Cycads, known as iron trees and living fossils, first appeared in the Paleozoic Permian period (古生代二叠纪) which began about 280 million years ago. The males of well-growing cycads bloom every year, and the female cycads, every two years. Covering more than 300 hectares, Panzhihua Cycads National Nature Reserve is home to more than 100,000 rare "Panzhihua cycads". It is of great significance in the study of flora (植物区系), phytogeography (植物地理), paleoclimate (古气候) and paleogeography (古地理).

 Section C   Oral Practices

Part One   Describing Pictures

Look at the following pictures and talk with your partner using the prompting words.

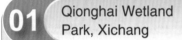 **01** Qionghai Wetland Park, Xichang

Prompting words: wetland; shallow lakes; along the bank; bird watching; ecofriendly

02 Luoji Mountain, Xichang

Prompting words: unique peaks; Buddha cave; rare stones; primary forest

03 Qinghe Waterfall, Yanbian

Prompting words: canyon; narrow and winding path; lush mountains; splash

04 Lushan Mountain, Xichang

Prompting words: Guangfu Temple; Museum of Yi; collection of stone tablets

05 Xichang Ancient City

Prompting words: ancient city wall; ancient building; lantern; a famous cultural city

06 Lingshan Temple, Mianning

Prompting words: Buddhist temple; monks; Buddhism; burn joss sticks

07 Huanglian Soil Forest, Xichang

Prompting words: unique shapes; crustal movement; erosion; masterpiece

08 Haita Scenic Spot, Miyi

Prompting words: artificial lake; wild fish; oxygen bar; peach blossom

Part Two   Group Discussion

Discuss the following topics with your partner.

1. **Everyone is proud of his/her hometown. When talking about his/her hometown with friends, he/she always begins with its history and famous stories. Talk about the history of your hometown, and your talk may include:**

    How many years of history does your hometown has?

    Is there any famous person from your hometown?

    Introduce to your friend and try to appeal them to know more details.

2. **While you want your friends to come to your hometown, there should be some beautiful places for them to visit. Introduce these places to your friends, and your talk may include:**

    Is there any famous scenic spot in your hometown?

    Show pictures to your friends, and tell them the feeling while you were there.

    Try to attract them to come to your hometown.

3. **Food is always attractive while inviting your friends to your hometown. Talk about food in your hometown, and your talk may include:**

    Is there any famous or delicious food in your hometown?

    Show pictures to your friends, or even bring some real food to the classroom, and try to describe how delicious they are!

4. **After all the effort you have done above, your friends must have accepted your invitation. You should be the guide while they are traveling in your hometown. Talk about the tourist route you design, and your talk may include:**

    Design a tourist route for your friends to travel in your hometown, make sure they can enjoy themselves there.

    Suppose you are a tour guide and your friends are tourists, start a conversation with the help of pictures.

5. **After all these preparations, design a presentation and present your hometown to your class as a tour guide. PPT should be used during your presentation.**

Section D   Extended Reading

Read the following passage that may help you better understand the topic of this unit.

The Taste of My Husband's Hometown —Roasted Chestnut

"Chestnuts roasting on an open fire" is the first line of *The Christmas Song*, one of my favorite holiday tunes growing up in America. Yet as a child, I never once roasted chestnuts at Christmas, let alone any other time of the year. Before I was born, a blight had devastated the vast majority of American chestnut trees, leaving me and most of my fellow countrymen strangers to the nut, apart from its mention in that timeless song.

In fact, it wasn't until I came to China that I truly understood the wonders of a freshly roasted chestnut, especially those gathered in the wild.

Years ago in September, I discovered that wild chestnut trees, a variety native to China, thrived in the hills of my husband's rural Zhejiang village, and were as close to us as the backyard of the family home. "See, there's a chestnut tree," he said, pointing out the window from his old bedroom to its trunk and branches just a few meters away from us. I couldn't believe this tree, a rare sight in America, actually grew beside the family garden.

So imagine my astonishment when, while hiking some remote hills near the village, I couldn't walk a few steps without stumbling over chestnuts that littered the ground. It was as if the heavens had decided to rain chestnuts upon the land, instead of water. My husband Jun had the foresight to suggest carrying along a few bags with us, and we began collecting these fall treasures as we meandered up and down the hills. Even though the sky was a melancholy gray, it felt like the sun had shined upon us that afternoon, thanks to the bounty of chestnuts we found and brought home with us.

The real magic, however, came from my mother-in-law, who helped me experience something close to that iconic line from *The Christmas Song* in her kitchen. Her wood-burning stove, with a wok on top, was the next best thing to an open fire. She roasted the chestnuts in the wok along with sweet osmanthus blossoms from the front yard, and filled the house with the intoxicating fragrance of flowers mingled with the caramel aroma of the nuts. I'll never forget the first time I inhaled it— it was like being all wrapped up in the warmth and coziness of the holidays, even though Dec. 25 was still months away.

That Christmassy feeling was only reinforced by the generous portion my mother-in-law sent up to our room, a huge silver bowl piled high with more roasted chestnuts than anyone could have consumed in one sitting. And even though lunch had finished a few hours ago, we couldn't resist the natural, sugary goodness of the snack.

Nowadays, whenever I imagine chestnuts, it's no longer Christmas that first comes to mind. Instead, my thoughts will turn to my husband's hometown—the hills scattered with wild chestnuts, the smell of them roasting in my mother-in-law's fire-powered wok, and the ambrosial flavor when eating them fresh from the stove. These memories have so completely saturated my brain that it's fall, not winter, that has become the season I most associate with chestnuts. So as much as I love that first line of *The Christmas Song*, perhaps it's time for someone—maybe me—to write the lyrics to an autumn melody that sings the praises of freshly roasted chestnuts in China.

我丈夫家乡的味道——烤栗子

"明火上烤着栗子"是《圣诞颂歌》的第一句歌词。这首兴起于美国的假日小曲是我最爱的歌曲之一。可是孩童时，我从未在圣诞节烤过栗子，更别提其他时间了。我出生之前，一场枯萎病摧毁了美国大部分的栗子树，致使我和大多数美国同胞对栗子感到陌生，更别提那首经典歌曲中所提及的烤栗子的场景了。

事实上，来到中国后我才真正体会到新鲜出炉的烤栗子的美妙之处，尤其是那些从野外采来的栗子。

　　多年前的一个九月，我发现在我丈夫的老家，浙江偏远农村的山丘上就生长着野生栗子树（一种原产于中国的品种），距离近得就跟长在自家后院似的。"你看，那儿有棵栗子树，"他从旧卧室里指着窗外离我们不过几米远的栗子树的躯干和枝条说。我不敢相信这棵树竟然就长在家里的小园子旁，因为这在美国很少见。

　　所以，当我在村子附近的偏僻小山徒步行走时，没走几步就会不可避免地踩到散落在地上的栗子，你可以想象我有多震惊。就好像老天爷决意要将雨水替换成"栗子"落在地上似的。我的先生军（音译）很有先见之明，他建议带些袋子在身边。我们在山间漫步的时候开始捡拾这些秋天的珍宝。我们捡了一大堆栗子带回家。多亏如此，尽管那个午后天空是阴郁的灰色，但却感觉阳光一直照耀着我们。

　　然而，真正令我感到神奇的是我的婆婆。她让我在厨房中体验到类似于《圣诞颂歌》中那句标志性歌词所描述的场景。她那烧柴火的炉子上架着一口锅，那是仅次于明火的好东西。婆婆把栗子放进锅子里烤，还加了些前院里香甜的桂花，屋子里充斥着桂花醉人的芬芳，其中还夹杂着栗子的焦糖香。我断不会忘了第一次吸入这芬芳的感受——就好像整个人都被假日的温暖和舒适包裹着，尽管距离圣诞节还有好几个月。

　　那种圣诞的气氛在婆婆给我们的房里送来一大份烤栗子时更加浓烈。一只银色大碗中，烤栗子堆得高高的，多得没有谁能坐在那儿一口气吃完。虽然刚吃完午饭不久，我们却抵挡不了这天然、甜蜜的营养小食。

　　如今，无论何时想起烤栗子，首先浮现在我脑海中的都不再是圣诞节。反之，我的思绪会飘向我丈夫的家乡——遍地散落着野栗子的小山丘，婆婆烧火的炒锅里烤着的栗子的香气，以及品尝刚出炉的栗子时的美味。这些记忆完完全全融入我的脑海中，以至于栗子让我最容易联想到的季节变成了秋天，而非冬天。既然我如此喜爱《圣诞颂歌》的第一句歌词，是时候有个人将这句词填进一首秋天的旋律里，以赞美中国的新鲜的烤栗子了，也许这个人就是我。

Unit 3
Food

Objectives

1. To know useful information about food
2. To practice dialogues about food
3. To describe pictures about food
4. To discuss topics about food

Warm-up Questions

1. What kind of cuisine do you like best? Why?
2. What's your favorite food? Why do you like it?
3. Do you often eat junk food? What makes you keep away from it? Or what makes you love it?

Section A   Getting Ready to Speak

Part One   Reading for Information

Read the following passages and get useful information about food.

Sichuan Cuisine

Sichuan cuisine is well-known all over the world. The cuisine features a wide range of materials, various seasonings, different cooking techniques and numerous tastes. Statistics show that the number of Sichuan dishes has surpassed 5,000. With a rich variety of strong flavors, Sichuan food is famous for its countless delicacies, dominated by peppery, chili flavors, and best known for being spicy-hot. Chili peppers and Sichuan pepper are used in many dishes, giving it a distinctively spicy taste, called ma (麻) in Chinese. It often leaves a slight numb sensation in the mouth. Thanks to the development of global trade, chili peppers were spread to Sichuan by Americans in the 18th century, which greatly influence flavor of Sichuan cuisine. Seasonings used in Sichuan cuisine include chili, garlic, cinnamon, dried orange peel, scallion, etc.

Hotpot

Hotpot is very popular in Chengdu and is known for its spicy and hot flavor. Although hotpot is considered as a Chongqing specialty by the locals, it has become famous and popular all over the country for a long time. A big pot is filled with hot spicy oil and surrounded by plates of raw meat and vegetables. Most of the pots used in hotpot are divided into two sections. One half is filled with the spicy oil, and the other is filled with a delicious broth for those who are not a big fan of spicy foods. As everyone knows, the taste of hotpot is determined by the broth. The kinds of broth of Chengdu hotpot are various. Although the main flavor is spicy, the different ingredients will make it taste different. There are over 10 varieties of Chengdu hotpot including hotpot with boiled mutton, hotpot with beer duck, fish head hotpot, medical herbs hotpot, etc. Besides the different kinds of broth of Chengdu hotpot, you can also choose the degree of spicy, which ranges from slightly to medium, and to very and super spicy.

Mapo Tofu

Mapo tofu is one of the most distinctive dishes with local flavor in China and also is popular all over the world. It started in Qing Dynasty, invented by a small restaurant owner Mrs. Chen. As Mrs. Chen had pockmark on her face and the pronunciation of pockmark in Chinese is Ma, the tofu she cooked is called Mapo tofu. Po is the address for old lady in Chinese. The ingredients used for Mapo tofu include tofu, broad bean paste, ginger, garlic, Sichuan pepper, garlic sprouts and minced beef. The brownish red minced beef and green garlic sprouts decorates the snow-white tender bean curd, making the dish look appetizing. The bland-tasting tofu is spiced up with a numbingly hot sauce, and barely perceptible grains of minced meat deliver a satisfactory crunch as the tofu melts in the mouth. It tastes spicy, numbing, aromatic and tender.

Part Two Dialogue Samples

Practice the following dialogues with your partner. Change the role when necessary.

Katie: What are the foods you can't stand?
Gilda: Number one would be chocolate.

Katie: Chocolate?
Gilda: Yes.

Katie: That's impossible!
Gilda: I don't like the feeling you have when you put a piece of chocolate inside your mouth. If I eat a piece of chocolate, I need to drink a lot of water.

Katie: Haha, I will gladly eat all your chocolate. If you have chocolate you don't want, I'm here.
Gilda: Good! It's weird because you know, chocolate is very popular as a gift. So, is there anything you don't like?

Katie: Well, yes. And every time I say I don't like it, I always get the same like, "What?" kind of reaction, but I don't like ice cream.
Gilda: What?

Katie: I don't like ice cream because it's too cold. I don't like cold food.
Gilda: Really? You don't know what you're missing. Ice creams are really, really tasty especially in summer.

Katie: Chocolate is really tasty, but chocolate ice cream is the worst.
Gilda: Well, you can try it.

Katie: No, thank you.

Gilda: Any other food that you don't like?

Katie: I don't like tomatoes. But I eat lots of pasta with tomato-flavored stuff in it. Just tomatoes by themselves are not something I enjoy.

Gilda: I can understand. I don't like garlic. But I like garlic in food as long as I don't see it or eat it and have this, the taste of garlic.

Katie: Once you've got the taste of garlic, you don't get rid of that for about three days.

Gilda: Exactly.

Katie: What do you usually eat for breakfast?

Gilda: Arepa (玉米饼). It's my daily breakfast in Venezuela.

Katie: What's that?

Gilda: Arepa is made of corn flour, and it looks like a hamburger. You can put anything you want inside and it's very tasty. Almost 95 percent of Venezuelans eat arepas every day.

Katie: I really want to try it.

Gilda: So, what about you? What about the breakfast in England?

Katie: Well, English breakfast is not that healthy. We have fried eggs, fried sausages, hash browns, like hash potatoes, beans, just everything fried and everything delicious. I can't live without that, but if I ate it every day, then I would probably not be able to leave my house because I would be so, so fat. Recently, I've been eating lots of tofu for breakfast.

Gilda: Oh, that's good.

Katie: Yeah. A little bit of tofu and a little bit of soy sauce for breakfast. It's a bit boring but really healthy.

Gilda: That sounds great. Nutritionally, tofu is low in calories while containing a relatively large amount of protein.

Katie: Exactly. I try to keep fit by taking in healthy food and exercising.

Gilda: Great!

Todd: Ivan, we are talking about your country, Indonesia. Can you recommend three Indonesian foods for people visiting your country?

Ivan: Oh, that can be a difficult question because we have various foods and it depends on your taste. I mean, if you like sweet food, we have a specialty for that and if you like spicy food, also there's a specialty for that. If I have to make a choice, the first is Nasi goreng (印尼炒饭). Nasi goreng is a kind of fried rice and I think it's quite popular anywhere else in the world.

Todd: It's called Nasi goreng?

Ivan: Nasi goreng, yeah. Nasi means rice, goreng means fry.

Todd: Oh, interesting.

Ivan: And then next one is Mi goreng (印尼炒面). Mi goreng is fried noodles. Mi means noodles and goreng means fry.

Todd: OK, so Mi goreng and Nasi goreng.

Ivan: Yeah, and the last one may be satay (沙茶酱烤肉).

Todd: What's that?

Ivan: It's kind of roast meat, and you can choose any meat you like, chicken, mutton, and so on. We usually have some kind of special sauce, basically it's ketchup, chili, salt and some ginger. You can dip the sauce when eating.

Todd: Oh, that sounds really tasty.

Ivan: Yeah, you'll like it if you try.

Part Three   Useful Expressions

Expressions below may help you talk about food.

Food materials

- bamboo shoots 竹笋
- bean sprout 豆芽
- bitter gourd 苦瓜
- broccoli 西兰花
- cabbage 卷心菜
- cane shoots 茭白
- cauli ower 菜花
- celery 芹菜
- Chinese cabbage 大白菜
- chives 韭黄
- coriander 香菜
- cucumber 黄瓜
- eggplant 茄子
- leek 韭菜
- lettuce 莴笋
- loofah 丝瓜
- lotus root 莲藕
- marrow 西葫芦
- prawn 对虾；大虾
- romaine 生菜
- sea-ear 鲍鱼
- spinach 菠菜
- string bean 四季豆
- white gourd 冬瓜

- white radish 白萝卜

Seasonings

- dark soy sauce 老抽
- garlic sprout 蒜苗
- light soy sauce 生抽
- oyster sauce 蚝油
- sesame oil 芝麻油
- Sichuan pepper 花椒
- spring onion 小葱

Cooking methods

- braise 烧；焖；烩；卤
- chop 切碎
- crush 捣碎，拍碎
- deep-fry 炸
- dice 切丁；切块
- shred 切丝
- simmer 煨
- slash 斜切
- slice 切片
- stew 煲；炖

Staple foods

- fried bread stick 油条
- rice noodles 米粉
- steamed bun 馒头
- steamed dumpling 蒸饺
- wonton 馄饨

- Yum! This chocolate pudding is so rich and creamy.
  太好吃了！这个巧克力布丁味道浓郁，口感细腻。

- Is that lemonade too sour?
  柠檬水是不是太酸了？

- The cake is too rich.
  这块蛋糕太油腻了。

- How about this pancake, chewy or crunchy/crispy?
  这个煎饼怎么样，是有嚼劲的还是脆的？

- Yuck, this black coffee is too bitter.
  哎呀，这黑咖啡太苦了。

- Can you show me a restaurant that serves tasty food at reasonable prices?
  你能告诉我一家菜好吃、价格又公道的餐馆吗？

- I'd like to reserve a table for two at seven tonight.
  我想订一张今天晚上 7 点的两人餐桌。

- How long to wait?
  要等多久？

- What would you like to eat/have?
  您想吃点什么？

- What do you want for dessert?
  您想吃什么甜点？

- Have you ordered yet?
  您点过菜了吗？

- What would you recommend?
  你推荐什么菜?

- What's your today's special?
  今天的特色菜是什么?

- The steak is very good today.
  今天的牛排很不错。

- How do you like your steak cooked, well-done or medium well?
  牛排您要几成熟,是全熟还是七分熟?

- How about a drink?
  喝一杯怎样?

- Do you want to have anything else?
  你还要吃别的东西吗?

- I don't feel like eating more.
  我不想再吃了。

- Please pass me the salt and pepper.
  请把盐和胡椒递给我.

- It's my treat./It's on me.
  今天我请客。

Section B Local Specialties

Look at the following pictures and get to know what they are about according to the describing words.

Panzhihua preserved meat (攀枝花油底肉): This is a famous specialty in Panzhihua, Sichuan Province. This meat is fragrant but not crispy, fat but not greasy, soft but not fleshy. The meat is usually stored in a jar filled with lard oil.

Rice-flour cake with sliced chicken (鸡火丝): It is a famous snack in the ancient city of Huili County, Liangshan Prefecture, Sichuan Province. The soup is mainly made from chicken, ham, and boiled bones. Pour the simmered soup onto the cooked rice-flour cake, and put a layer of chicken on it. This snack is nutritious and delicious.

Drunk shrimp (醉虾): As the name implies, the live shrimps are soaked in rice wine, and they will be drunken soon. Put the ice cubes in a glassware, then add in the live shrimps, garlic, ginger, light soy sauce, vinegar, a little sugar, red peppers and spring onions, and pour the rice wine to make the shrimps fully soaked and then cover the glassware. After ten minutes, a flavorful dish is served.

Chunked meat (坨坨肉): It is made of beef, mutton, pork or chicken. First, cut the meat into large pieces. Then boil them fully and pour the garlic juice on them. Finally, add in salt, chili and Sichuan pepper powder. This dish gives people the feeling of eating a chunk of meat while taking a bowlful of drinking!

Qinghe tofu pudding (清河豆花): This is a famous specialty in Yanbian County, Panzhihua, Sichuan Province. There is no gypsum or bittern added, so the tofu pudding tastes not bitter but a little sweet. You can add some local spicy seasoning when eating.

Yanbian rice noodles with mutton (盐边羊肉米线): The mutton in the rice noodles is locally produced. More than ten flavors of Chinese herbal medicine are added in to remove the odor of mutton.

Copper hotpot (铜火锅): It is a specialty of Miyi County, Panzhihua, Sichuan Province. There are three layers of foods. At the bottom is purple yam, sweet potato, cabbage head, lotus root, potatoes and carrots. Upward is the black-bone chicken, pork ribs, duck and bacon; on the top are the big pork balls.

Water centipede (爬沙虫): They are known as ginseng in the soil and are extremely nutritious. They are often dipped in egg and bean paste and fried in a pan. This dish is fragrant, spicy and delicious, with a long aftertaste.

 Section C   Oral Practices

Part One   Describing Pictures

Look at the following pictures and talk with your partner using the prompting words.

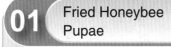 **01** Fried Honeybee Pupae

炸蜂蛹

Prompting words: fry; high in protein; nutritious; crisp; tender

02 Buckwheat Pancake

苦荞饼

Prompting words: traditional Miyi food; golden yellow; fragrant; a bit bitter; good for health

03 Fried Bacon with Kapok

桂花炒腊肉

Prompting words: kapok stamens; bacon; edible value

04 Grass Jelly

凉粉

Prompting words: bean jelly; creamy; appetizing; refreshment

05 Fried Fresh Termite Mushroom

香炒鸡枞菌

Prompting words: termite mushroom; protein; amino acids; vitamin

06 Yanbian Tuotuo Chicken

盐边坨坨鸡

Prompting words: cold dish; green pepper; chili; chewy

07 Beef Salad

凉拌牛肉

Prompting words: cold dish; hot and spicy; fresh Sichuan pepper

08 Barbecue in a Brazier

火盆烧烤

Prompting words: alpine potatoes and corns; roast suckling pig; corn wine; pickle; special sauce

Part Two   Group Discussion

Discuss the following topics with your partner.

1. **Describe a dish.**

    How is the dish cooked?

    Who do you usually cook for?

2. **Talk about Eight Major Cuisine Types（八大菜系）in China.**

    List the Eight Major Cuisine Types in China.

    What are the typical features of each cuisine?

    What are the representative dishes of each cuisine?

    Which cuisine do you like best?

    Can you describe one of the typical dishes about its flavor, color or cooking method?

3. **Talk about unusual food.**

    Have you ever tried any unusual foods or drinks? Do you like them?

    What unusual foods would you like to try? Why?

    What food from your hometown might be unusual to visitors?

4. **Talk about the food you eat.**

    What foods do you usually eat?

    Is there any food you don't like?

    What's your opinion on "We are what we eat."?

5. **Talk about eating habit.**

    Which do you like more: healthy food or junk food? Why?

    Can you tell us the names of unhealthy foods (junk foods) as many as possible?

    Which foods do you think are healthy?

    How often do you eat in a restaurant? (How often do you eat out?)

    What food do you cook the most often?

Section D   Extended Reading

Read the following passage that may help you better understand the topic of this unit.

Must-Try Foods of the World

Safety is the usual choice for global travelers when faced with a menu of unknown dishes. But a great meal transcends all cultural boundaries, and sharing the food of your host country is the best way to connect with its people and culture.

China

In Beijing the restaurants in the alleyways of Qian Men are renowned for hotpot, or huo guo (火锅). Here you'll find the streets are lined with boiling pots filled with soup ingredients. Its excellent selections range from Mongolian specialties—best known for lamb and mutton dishes— and spicy Sichuan hotpot.

Some 600-plus miles away, Shanghai is best known for its street food, especially soup dumplings. But don't stop there, sheng jian bao, steamed pork bun, makes for a perfect for snack, while jian bing, egg-based crepes with a bean sauce or chili smear, is a famous local breakfast.

Brazil

No culinary trip here is complete without a visit to the state of Bahia. First thing to order: moqueca de peixe, a fish (and sometimes shrimp) stew made with tomatoes and coconut milk. For a satisfying weekend lunch—not unlike American brunch—feijoada, a heavy stew of beans, meat and sausage, served with rice, can be found all over Brazil. If you're looking for something lighter, fresh grilled fish with tomato-and-onion salad coupled with a couple of Brahma beers is a perfect beach meal.

India

Word of advice: avoid street food. Try to score an invite to a local dinner table rather than settle for street vendors. Many locals are vegetarian, but Indian cuisine includes a variety of delicious meat and seafood. Grilled minced lamb, seekh kebabs, are the staple of Tandoori cooking, while the nation's coastal regions are renowned for masala (spiced) fish or prawns. Natives advise caution when eating seafood during the monsoon months of June to August due to the increase in water-borne diseases.

While India conjures up images of curries, local specialties are worth digging around for. In North India, never say no to chaat or paani-puri. These delicious crispy crackers are dressed up with condiments of the sweet and spicy variety. If you're in the south, don't leave without trying fresh coconut. Traveling tappers climb coconut trees, tap the fruit's blossom and decant the sap into a bottle. As the day progresses, the liquid becomes increasingly intoxicating, transforming from a light, fizzy drink mid-morning and fermenting into a seriously strong alcoholic drink by evening.

Italy

Pizza not exotic enough for you? The pizza in Naples has a "DOP" stamp of approval from the Italian government to authenticate it. The ingredients are simply dough and a rich marinara sauce with oregano. Locals say there's something in the water density in Naples that guarantees you will never have a pizza like it anywhere else in the world.

If you're lucky enough to be around during the autumn truffle season, try uova con tartufi— fried eggs with truffle oil. It can't be found on restaurant menus, but chefs from Tuscany and Umbria will know exactly what you mean if you ask for it.

Japan

You can get great sushi almost everywhere, so when you're in Japan it's worth trying other delicacies. Okonomiyaki, a savory pancake (or Japanese pizza) from Hiroshima, is made with batter, vegetables, seaweed, meat, a sweet sauce resembling Worcestershire, and Japanese mayonnaise. Other regional delicacies include anago-meshi, or sea eel rice, and tonkatsu ramen from Hakata, a pork-bone white soup with ramen noodles.

Russia

The best meals are worth the money in Russia. If you see solyanka on the menu, don't hesitate to order. This salty, sour and often spicy soup combined with meat or fish and topped with smetana, Russian sour cream, is delicious.

Borscht and pelmeni (dumplings) are ubiquitously Russian, but experiment with different varieties, such as salmon and wild mushroom pelmeni. Borscht can be spiced up with roasted apples and smoked goose breast. If you find the time, a culinary side trip to Georgia or Armenia in search of Azerbaijaini plov, a spiced rice dish cooked with meat and dried fruit, is worth the journey.

世界各国必尝美食

对于环球旅行者来说，当看到菜单上面都是自己不知道的菜肴时，他们往往会选择自己认为安全的食物。但是美食是超越所有文化界限的，品尝当地的食物是与当地人交流、融入当地文化的最佳方式。

中国

北京前门胡同里的餐馆以火锅而闻名。在这里，你会发现街上到处都是装满汤底的沸腾锅子。可供选择的美味火锅有内蒙古特色火锅——最有名的是羔羊肉和羊肉火锅，还有辛辣的四川火锅。

大概600多英里以外的上海美食以街边小吃而闻名，特别是灌汤包。不过可不只有灌汤包，还有生煎包——一种蒸熟的猪肉包——是一种很棒的小吃，而煎饼——以鸡蛋为主料做成的薄饼，抹上豆瓣酱或辣椒酱——是当地非常有名的早餐。

巴西

如果没有去巴伊亚州，那么你在巴西的美食之旅就不完整。第一道要点的菜是炖鱼，就是将鱼（有时是虾）和西红柿以及椰子汁一起炖。像美国的早午餐一样，丰盛的周末午餐——巴西炖菜，就是把豆子、肉和香肠一起炖，再配上米饭——在整个巴西都能品尝到。如果你想要品尝一些较清淡的菜肴，鲜嫩的烤鱼、西红柿洋葱沙拉，再配上几瓶博浪啤酒，简直是一顿完美的海滩大餐。

印度

忠告：不要吃街边食物。尽量获得当地人的邀请到其家中品尝美食，而不要在街边摊贩那里品尝。许多当地人都是素食主义者，不过印度菜肴中囊括了许多美味的肉和海鲜。烤羊肉卷——烤制而成的切碎的羔羊肉——是采用泥炉炭火烹饪法烹制而成的常见食物，而这个国家沿海地区的美食则以马萨拉（辣味）鱼或对虾而出名。当地人建议在 6 月到 8 月这三个季风月份要谨慎品尝海鲜，因为水传播疾病会增加。

虽然提到印度就会让人想起咖喱，但当地有许多其他特色美食值得你搜寻。在北印度，一定要吃 chaat 或 paani-puri。这些美味松脆的点心可以加各种甜味和辣味调味品。如果你在印度南部，那么就不能不品尝一下新鲜的椰子。流动采集工人爬上椰子树，轻轻地敲开椰壳，将椰子汁倒入一个瓶子里。放上一天，椰子汁会变得越来越醇香，上午还是清淡、有气泡的饮料，到了晚上就发酵成浓烈的酒精饮料。

意大利

对你来说，比萨不够"意大利"吗？那不勒斯的比萨有意大利政府的原产地保护认证标志以证明它的品质。它的原材料就只有生面团和加了牛至叶粉、味道浓郁的番茄大蒜调味汁。当地人说那不勒斯的水密度有点不一般，这能保证你所品尝的比萨与世界上其他任何地方的比萨都不同。

如果你足够幸运是在秋季松露季节前后来到意大利，那么一定要尝尝加了松露油的煎蛋——uova con tartufi。虽然餐厅的菜谱上没有这种煎蛋，但如果你点这道菜的话，来自托斯卡纳区和翁布里亚的厨师们肯定知道你点的是什么。

日本

你几乎在任何地方都能吃到很棒的寿司，所以到了日本不妨尝尝其他美食吧。御好烧是来自广岛的一种好吃的薄饼（也可称为"日本比萨"），它是由面糊、蔬菜、海藻、肉、类似伍斯特沙司的甜酱和日本蛋黄酱做成的。其他日本地方美食料理还有鳗鱼寿司或鳗鱼饭、博多豚骨拉面——就是在猪脊骨高汤中下入拉面。

俄罗斯

在俄罗斯，上等的美食值得你花钱品尝。如果你在菜单上看到酸辣浓汤，那你一定要点。这个咸、酸，通常还有点辣的汤里有肉或鱼，上面还加了"斯美塔那"（一种俄罗斯酸奶油），非常美味。

罗宋汤和俄罗斯饺子"佩尔米尼"在俄罗斯非常常见，不过你也可以尝尝各种不同的口味，比如鲑鱼和野蘑菇水饺。罗宋汤可以用烘烤过的苹果和熏鹅脯来提味。如果你有时间的话，可以顺便去游览一下格鲁吉亚或亚美尼亚，品尝一种用肉和果脯烹制而成的香米饭——Azerbaijaini plov，绝对不虚此行。

Unit 4
Leisure Time & Travel

Objectives

1. To know useful information about some travel destinations in China
2. To practice dialogues about travel
3. To describe pictures of scenic spots
4. To discuss topics about leisure time and travel

Warm-up Questions

1 Do you like travel? Why?

2 Which city do you like to travel best? Why?

3 Do you have any impressive experience when traveling?

Section A　Getting Ready to Speak

Part One　Reading for Information

Read the following passages and get useful information about some travel destinations in China.

Xi'an City

Xi'an, meaning "West, Peace", the capital of Shanxi Province, is located at the center of Guanzhong Plain, a flood plain created by the eight surrounding rivers and streams in northwestern China. The city has an average elevation of 400 meters above sea level. The Wei River provides potable water to the city.

It is one of the Four Great Ancient Capitals in China, serving as the capital of several dynasties in Chinese history, including Zhou, Qin, Han, Sui, and Tang. Xi'an is the starting point of the Silk Road and home to the Terracotta Army of Emperor Qin Shi Huang.

Since the 1990s, as part of the economic revival of inland China especially for the central and northwestern regions, Xi'an has re-emerged as an important cultural, industrial and educational center, with facilities for research and development, national security and space exploration programs. As of 2018, Xi'an has a population of more than 10 million. It is one of the most populous cities in western China.

Xi'an hosted the 2011 World Horticultural Exposition, from April 28 to October 28, 2011.

Leshan Giant Buddha

Leshan Giant Buddha, with a height of 71 meters, is the largest Buddha figure in the world. The Giant Buddha's head alone has a height of 14.7 meters, with 1,021 nubs depicting hair, and the ear is 6.72 meters long, the eye socket 3.3 meters wide, and the nose 5.33 meters long. Other key dimensions include the shoulders at 24 meters wide, the index finger at 8.3 meters long, and the lap, which can seat a hundred people, at 9 meters wide and 11 meters long. In back of the figure's head is a cleverly devised set of crisscrossing drain channels such that no water can accumulate here and weaken the mountain's "hold" on the figure, though some water damage to the Giant Buddha has occurred, namely on its lap area. The fact that the Giant Buddha remains in excellent overall condition after more than a thousand years can to a large extent be attributed to the ingeniousness of its drainage system. Leshan Giant Buddha is a cultural treasure not only to the people of China, but also to the world at large.

Jiuzhaigou Valley

The Jiuzhaigou Valley Scenic and Historic Interest Area is a reserve of exceptional natural beauty with spectacular jagged alpine mountains soaring above coniferous forest around a fairyland landscape of crystal-clear, strange-colored blue, green and purplish pools, lakes, waterfalls, limestone terraces, caves and other beautiful features. These include a number of karst formations; indeed, the area is a "natural museum" for alpine karst hydrology and research. Covering 72,000 hectares in the northern part of Sichuan Province, Jiuzhaigou preserves a series of important forest ecosystems including old-growth forests which provide important habitat for numerous threatened species of plants and animals, including the giant panda, snub-nosed monkeys, takin and so on. Attaining heights of 4,752 meters in the southern Minshan Mountains, Jiuzhaigou also contains an important number of well-preserved quaternary glacial remnants with great scenic value. In 1992, it was listed as a world cultural heritage site by the UNESCO.

Though with a high altitude, Jiuzhaigou has a humid climate unlike the extreme weather as in other high-altitude region, such as Tibetan Plateau, which should be owned to the rich natural resource, especially wild forests and rivers. It has lots of sunny days all year around, a cool summer and less wind in winter. The average temperature in Jiuzhaigou is from 9 to 18 centigrade. The total annual rainfall there is 761 mm. Summer and autumn are two best seasons to tour Jiuzhaigou when all attractions are available for visiting. In summer days, the plentiful water replenishes every rivers, lakes and waterfalls for you to enjoy the stunning waterscape. The most beautiful scenery comes in autumn especially October when the entire Jiuzhaigou is filled with diverse colors. Besides, the weather is very pleasant in autumn days.

Part Two   Dialogue Samples

Practice the following dialogues with your partner. Change the role when necessary.

Ruby: Good evening.

Receptionist: Good evening, ma'am. May I help you?

Ruby: Yes. I'd like to check in, please. I made a reservation a week ago under the name of Ruby Hsu, H-S-U, for three nights from tonight. And here is my confirmation slip.

Receptionist: Thank you, Miss Hsu. A second, please. Oh, yes, we've got your reservation. It is a single room with bath. Is it correct?

Ruby: Yeah, correct.

Receptionist: Then, please fill out this form, Miss Hsu.

Ruby: Sure. (Fill out the registration card) Is this OK?

Receptionist: Yes, thank you. Your room number is 666 and here is your room key. Just leave your baggage here and I'll get the porter to carry it up right away.

Ruby: Thank you very much.

Receptionist: My pleasure.

James: Excuse me.

Receptionist: Yes. Good evening, sir. What can I do for you?

James: Good evening. I want... I mean I'd like a room for tonight. Do you have any vacancy?

Receptionist: Oh, I'm terribly sorry, but we are all booked out.

James: Pardon me?

Receptionist: I mean that we have rented out all the rooms today.

James: Not even one left?

Receptionist: No. I'm sorry.

James: That's OK. Thanks anyway.

Ruby: Check out, please.

Cashier: Your room number, please?

Ruby: Oh, the room number is 666 and here is the key.

Cashier: Thank you. Did you enjoy your stay here?

Ruby: Very much. The room was comfy and the service was great.

Cashier: Thank you. Our pleasure. Here is your check. The total is three hundred and forty-five dollars, tax included. How would you like to pay?

Ruby: Can I pay by traveler's check?

Cashier: Of course. Can I have your passport, please?

Ruby: Here you are.

Cashier: Thank you. That's all done and hope you visit next time.

Waiter: Good evening. Please take your seats, gentlemen. Here are the menus. Would you like to drink something first?

Customer A: I'll have a cup of coca cola with ice.

Waiter: What about you, sir?

Customer B: A cup of apple juice, please.

Waiter: Okay. Here we are. Coca cola with ice and apple juice. Are you ready to order now, gentlemen?

Customer A: No, we are still looking at the menu. Could you recommend something for the main course?

Waiter: Certainly. The T-bone steak is very good. I would suggest you to try it.

Customer A: I love beef steak. I'll have the T-bone steak.

Waiter: How would you like it cooked?

Customer A: Medium well.

Waiter: And what would you like for your appetizer?

Customer A: I'll have salad and the baked salmon.

Waiter: Thank you, sir. What about you, sir?

Customer B: I want salad. What is this?

Waiter: It's lamb cooked with herbs and served with spaghetti.

Customer B: Sounds good, I'll try it.

Waiter: Mashed potato, boiled potato or baked potato?

Customer B: Mashed.

Waiter: Which sauce would you like? We have black pepper sauce, red wine sauce, onion sauce, vanilla sauce, BBQ sauce and mushroom sauce.

Customer B: Red wine sauce, please.

Waiter: Anything more, sir?

Customer A: No, that's enough. Thank you.

(After a few minutes)

Customer A: Can I have the check, please?

Waiter: Of course.

Customer B: George. Let's split the bill.

Customer A: No, it's my treat tonight.

Waiter: Cash or charge, sir?

Customer A: Charge, please. Put it on my American Express.

Broadcast: The plane is about to take off. Please turn off any communication equipment.

A: (Take B on his shoulder) Hey, guy. Please power off your phone, or it will be dangerous.

B: What? What will be dangerous?

A: The plane is about to take off. We should do as we are required. It's the common sense you know.

B: Oh, sorry. It's my first time to travel by plane. I don't know that.

A: Never mind. I was just like you during my first time. You say it's your first time to travel by plane, right?

B: Yes, I like traveling very much. But I always choose to take trains if the destination is not far away. Just now, I sent a micro-blog to express my exciting feeling.

A: Understand. Maybe I can give you some suggestions. When the plane is flying, you will have some ache about your ears. Take it easy. It can be fine after several minutes. And you can ask flight attendants for help at any time.

B: I remember. It's very kind of you. Thank you very much.

A: It doesn't matter. The captain will broadcast some suggestions, and you should pay attention to that. Hope you have a happy trip.

B: Thank you and have a happy time, too.

Part Three   Useful Expressions

Expressions below may help you talk about travel.

- airsick 晕机
- backpacker 背包客
- bathing beach 海滨浴场
- carry-on baggage 随身行李
- cottage 小别墅
- deep-sea fishing 深海垂钓
- deposit 定金
- economy/tourist class 经济舱
- ecotourism 生态旅游
- excess baggage charges 超重行李费
- expedition 探险
- family suite 家庭套房
- first class 头等舱
- fish pedicure 鱼疗
- five-star hotel 五星级酒店
- free baggage allowance 免费行李额
- free walker 自由行
- guesthouse 家庭旅馆
- historical heritage 历史遗产
- honeymoon suite 蜜月套房
- hot spring bath 泡温泉

- independent traveler 旅游散客
- international/domestic fight 国际/国内航班
- junior suite 普通套房
- lodge 乡间小屋；旅馆
- low season 淡季
- luggage depository 行李存放处
- luggage/baggage claim 行李认领处
- mini suite 小型套房
- outbound trip 出境游
- peak season 旺季
- penthouse suite 顶楼套房
- registered/checked luggage 托运行李
- return journey/round trip 往返旅行
- riverboat excursion 乘船短途游览
- round-trip/return-trip ticket 返程票
- scheduled ight 定期航班
- single ticket 单程票
- sleeper 卧铺
- stopover 中途停留
- taxi pick-up point 出租车乘车点
- time-share 分时度假
- transfer passenger 中转乘客
- vacation tour 度假旅游
- wake-up service 叫醒服务

- I'd like a single room with bath and a good view.
  我想要一间视野好并且带浴室的单人间。

- Do you have a double room overlooking the sea?
  你们有没有俯瞰海景的双人间呢?

- I'd like to pay by cash/traveler's check.
  我想用现金/旅行支票付款。

- You must obey all the traffic rules.
  你要遵守所有的交通规则。

- What's on the schedule for today?
  今天有哪些日程安排?

- Where is the tourist information center?
  请问旅游问讯处在哪里?

- How much does it cost to the city center by taxi?
  乘出租车到市中心需要多少钱?

- May I have a city map?
  可以给我一张市区地图吗?

- Take me to this address, please.
  请载我去这个地址。

- How long does it take to go to the city center?
  到市中心需要多长时间?

- How long does it take to get there on foot?
  步行到那里需要多长时间?

- Could you show me the way on the map?
  你能在地图上给我指路吗?

- I'll arrive late, but please keep my reservation.
  我会晚一点到达，请保留我预订的房间。

- I made a reservation in Chengdu.
  我在成都已预订房间。

- Do you accept credit card (traveler's check)?
  这里可以使用信用卡（旅行支票）吗?

- Could you keep my valuables?
  是否可代为保管贵重物品?

- Can I have a card with the hotel's address?
  是否可给我一张有旅馆地址的名片?

- Where is the nearest subway station?
  最近的地铁站在哪里?

- Can I get a ticket for the sight-seeing bus here?
  是否可在此购买观光巴士票?

Section B   Local Specialties

Look at the following pictures and get to know what they are about according to the describing words.

Yishala Village (迤沙拉村), China's largest Yi (彝) village, known as the first Yi village in the world, is located in the deep mountains of Jinsha River at the southern end of Panzhihua, Sichuan Province. There are more than 600 families living there, of which more than 400 families are highly centralized on a small hillside. Due to long-term multi-ethnic exchanges and integration, unique folk culture and architectural culture have been formed there.

Mount Emei is located seven kilometers southwest of Emei City. It stretches more than 200 kilometers from south to north, and its main peak, 3,099 meters above the sea level, is described as Beauty Under Heaven. Mount Emei is one of the most famous Buddhist mountains in China, and listed as world heritage by the UNESCO in 1996.

Rafting training base, located by the Jinsha River, is well-known for the international rafting festival, and is the ideal place for challenging and adventurous activities. The competition covers a number of events, such as speed racing, obstacle racing and rally racing, and other comprehensive sports projects.

Ertan National Forest Park (二滩国家森林公园) has beautiful natural scenery with green mountains, deep canyons, good habitat for wild animals, and spectacular man-made structure. Ertan Hydro-Power Station, 33 kilometers away from the intersection of Yalong River and Jinsha River in Panzhihua City, with an installed capacity of 3.3 million kilowatts and an annual generating capacity of 17 billion kilowatts, ranks first in China.

Located in the northwest corner of Yanbian County (盐边县), Gesala Ecotourism Area (格萨拉生态旅游区), covers an area of 594.23 square kilometers, with diverse vegetation and biological resources, natural landscape, primitive forests, azalea, underground caves, and alpine meadow, and is honored as "natural geological museum". With its multi-ethnic culture, tourists can learn about Yi people's customs and beautiful legend there.

Longtan Cave (龙潭溶洞), located in Baima Township (白马镇), is the workmanship of nature. The stalactites, formed by the slow dropping of water, contain various minerals. Various forms of stalactites hang from the ceilings of the cave, or rise up from the ground, in strange shape, illuminated by light. And there are large and small waterfalls in the cave.

Zhuhu Park (竹湖园) is surrounded by green mountains. Small bridges and running water, green trees and pavilions, are at the entrance of the park. There are groups of sculptures, made of ochre stone, symbolizing the bright sunshine of Panzhihua City.

There are hot springs in a five-star hotel in Panzhihua. You can enjoy the hot spring in various ways there: public pool, private pool, family pool, or even a small spring pool in your room. The hot spring water there smells like bad eggs because of the sulfur element it contains. However, this kind of smelly water is quite good for people's health.

Section C   Oral Practices

Part One   Describing Pictures

Look at the following pictures and talk with your partner using the prompting words.

01 Daheishan Forest Park

Prompting words: dense forest; arrow bamboo forest; sunrise; rosy clouds; sea of clouds

02 Huilongwan Cave Site

Prompting words: the Old Stone Age; bone fossils; primitive culture; microlith culture

03 Flower Sea of Panzhihua

Prompting words: Ashuda Village (阿署达村); flowers; dancing butterflies; pretty weather

04 Baipo Mountain Provincial Nature Reserve

Prompting words: Miyi County; musk deer; evergreen broad-leaf forest; rare animals; unique landform

05 Puda Sunshine International Holiday Resort

Prompting words: leisure tourism; resort for health care; amusement park; folk culture villages

06 European Camp

Prompting words: Little United Nations; Ertan Hydro-Power Station; foreign experts; construction; villas; rock climbing

07 Malu Village-Hongbi Beach Natural Scenic Spot

Prompting words: natural scenic spot; Manwang Cave (蛮王洞); abundant rainfall; mountains and meadows

08 Wuben Township

Prompting words: "peach blossom village"; "ancient country of Ura" (乌拉古国); pleasant climate

Part Two   Group Discussion

Discuss the following topics with your partner.

1. **Talk about the most impressive mountain climbing you have ever had.**

    Which famous mountain have you ever climbed?

    With whom did you climb or did you climb alone?

    When did you climb it?

    What have you learned from this experience?

2. **Talk about taking a bath in the hot spring.**

    What famous hot springs do you know in China?

    What are the benefits of taking a bath in the hot spring?

    Have you ever taken a bath in the hot spring? If yes, can you talk about your feelings?

3. **Talk about picnic or barbecue.**

    Have you ever had a picnic or barbecue? Did you like such kind of activities?

    Where and when would you go to have a picnic or barbecue? Why?

    With whom would you go to have a picnic or barbecue?

4. **Talk about planting trees.**

    Is planting trees useful? Why?

    Have you ever planted trees? If yes, what kind of trees have you planted?

    Where would you like to plant trees?

    How do you understand the Chinese saying "Lucid waters and lush mountains are invaluable assets." (绿水青山就是金山银山。)?

5. **Talk about plans for holiday.**

    What do you like to do on holiday: staying at home or traveling? Why?

    Can you list the places you have visited as many as possible?

    Among the places you have visited, which one do you like best? Why?

    In which season will you prefer to travel? Why?

Section D   Extended Reading

Read the following passage that may help you better understand the topic of this unit.

The Favorite Tourist Destinations in Summer

Lake Lucerne, Switzerland

The medieval city Lucerne is choked with tour buses, but new developments around the spacious lake it sits on (called Lake Lucerne by tourists but known as Vierwaldstättersee to locals) promise to thin crowds and offer accessible doses of authentic Swiss Alps.

Kauai, Hawaii, America

The island's ubiquitous aerial tours do deliver jaw-dropping views of the towering Na Pali Coast sea cliffs, cascading waterfalls, and other blockbuster locations. But plunging deep into the Garden Island's wild side requires hitting a trail. Marked hiking paths lead on to the floor of Waimea Canyon, through the shallow bogs of Alakai Swamp, and across unbelievably lush landscapes.

Basilicata, Italy

These are caves, beaches and more in Italy's secret southern region. This is a chance to visit Italy's southern region before the world catches on. Between the heel that is Puglia and the toe that is Calabria, you will find Basilicata, the arch of Italy's foot. Despite a storied and ancient past, the region has been overlooked in modern times. Easily Italy's best-kept secret, Basilicata is revered for beautiful beaches, ancient towns and a dearth of organized crime.

Qinghai Lake, Qinghai, China

Qinghai Lake is China's largest inland saltwater lake, with an area of more than 4,400 square kilometers. As a paradise for birdwatchers and cyclists, the blue water is fascinating. Every summer many cyclists will come for Tour de Qinghai Lake International Cycling Race.

Pudacuo National Park, Shangri-la, Yunnan, China

Pudacuo is the first national park in China to meet the criteria set by the World Conservation Union. More than 20% of the country's plant species and around one-third of its mammal and bird species call this wetland plateau home. Photographers especially love the area's many types of orchids and China's highly endangered black-necked cranes.

Xinjiang, China

This is a journey into some of the most sublime landscapes on earth. Xinjiang is increasingly attracting visitors for its extraordinary natural beauty and fascinating history and culture. In short, a visit to Chinese Taklimakan Desert makes for an exploration of China's past and its cultural diversity, or simply a journey into some of the most sublime landscapes on earth.

In terms of natural beauty, there are few places like Xinjiang. Not only is it home to the spectacular Altai and Kunlun Mountains and the lush Nalati and Bayanbulak Grasslands, but also the vast and rugged Taklimakan Desert. There are few places in China and around the world that have such a rich natural landscape as Xinjiang.

With regard to cultural diversity, Xinjiang is home to many different ethnic groups including Uyghur, Hui, Kazakh, Tajik and so on. The visitors have the opportunity to experience each of these amazing cultures, including their unique foods and customs.

夏季最火的旅游目的地

瑞士　四森林州湖

中世纪城市卢塞恩挤满了观光巴士，但它所处的广阔湖泊（游人把它唤作卢塞恩湖，当地人称之为"四森林州湖"）周围正在开发新的旅游景点，届时将大大分散如织的游人，让你领略纯正的瑞士阿尔卑斯风光。

美国　夏威夷考艾岛

从空中全角度观赏这座岛屿，那景观美得令人窒息，你能鸟瞰纳巴利海岸海崖、倾泻而下的瀑布以及超级大片级别的风景。但如果要深入探寻这个花园岛屿的野生风貌，则需要另辟蹊径。标识好的登山路线能指引游客到达威美亚峡谷，一路可以饱览阿拉基沼泽的浅浅泥塘和令人难以置信的醉人风光。

意大利　巴斯利卡塔

神秘的意大利南部有洞穴、海滩等美景，却鲜为人知。趁世人还未发现这片美丽的土地，不妨赶紧去意大利南部一探究竟。意大利在地图上好似一只靴子，普利亚区是它的鞋跟，卡拉布里亚区则是鞋尖，而中间的足弓地带就是巴斯利卡塔区。尽管这片地区传说众多，历史悠久，如今却依然鲜为人知。可以说，巴斯利卡塔地区是意大利最大的秘密。这儿有风景优美的沙滩，还有古老的小镇，别担心，这里没有黑帮组织。

中国青海　青海湖

青海湖是中国最大的内陆咸水湖，面积达 4 400 多平方千米。这里是观鸟者和骑行者的天堂，蓝色的湖水异常迷人。每年夏季都有一群自行车手聚集到这里参加环青海湖国际公路自行车赛。

中国云南 香格里拉普达措国家公园

　　普达措是中国首个符合世界自然保护联盟保护标准的国家级公园。这个湿地高原养育着中国超过 20% 的植物以及大约 1/3 的哺乳动物和鸟类。摄影家们喜爱这里种类繁多的兰花和国家一级保护动物黑颈鹤。

中国新疆

　　这是一次探寻地球极致风景之旅。 新疆凭借其独特的自然景观及迷人的历史与文化，吸引着越来越多的旅行者。简言之，一趟塔克拉玛干沙漠之旅，既可以领略极致的自然美景，也可以探寻中国的历史及其多样的文化。

　　在自然风光方面，少有地方能像新疆一样。那里不仅有惊人的壮丽山川（阿尔泰山和昆仑山）、草原（那拉提草原和巴音布鲁克草原），还有广阔崎岖的塔克拉玛干沙漠。在中国，乃至全世界，都少有地方能像新疆一样，有如此丰富多样的自然景观。

　　在文化多样性方面，新疆是多种民族聚居的地区，包括维吾尔族、回族、哈萨克族、塔吉克族等。游客们可以体验这些令人惊叹的文化，包括其独特的美食与习俗。

Unit 5
Shopping

Objectives

1. To know useful information about shopping
2. To practice dialogues about shopping
3. To describe pictures of specialties you can buy in Sichuan
4. To discuss topics about shopping

Warm-up Questions

1. Do you like shopping? Where do you often go for shopping?
2. Do you compare prices when shopping? Do you often ask for a discount?
3. What do you pay attention to when you go shopping?

 Section A   Getting Ready to Speak

Part One   Reading for Information

Read the following passages and get useful information about shopping.

 Women of Xiamen Spending $115 Million in a Day

The women in Xiamen, Fujian Province spent nearly 800 million yuan ($115 million) on Nov. 11, 2018, the largest online shopping festival in China, taking up 57 percent of the sum of local residents' consumption. Statistics from Alibaba shows that Apple products are Xiamen residents' most favorite and Apple mobile phones are particularly popular among them. Besides, sanitary ware products, woolen coats and flat panel televisions are also their favorite products.

More efficient express service is enjoyed by Chinese consumers during the busy shopping festival since many of them can receive their parcels several hours after they place their orders. The Double Eleven Festival was devised ten years ago by Alibaba as Singles Day, an anti-Valentine's day of big discounts at its e-commerce malls, and their all-day trading volume set another record with 213.5 billion yuan this year. It only took one hour 46 minutes 26 seconds for this online platforms' trading volume to exceed 100 billion yuan this year, approximately seven hours faster than last year.

Black Friday

The US holiday shopping season has officially begun, with shoppers crowding stores for post-Thanksgiving sales in a yearly event nicknamed "Black Friday", which is the day many stores sharply discount high-priced items such as electronics and the latest new toys. Its name signifies retailers' expectations of high sales, as profits were once recorded in account books in black ink, while losses were recorded in red. Stores also open their doors hours earlier than usual, which helps foster excitement among bargain hunters. Black Friday is one of the most important days for retail chains because it indicates what they can expect during the next month of holiday shopping—their most lucrative time of year. But not everyone is in favor of the phenomenon. Protesters with the anti-capitalist Occupy Wall Street movement were encouraging people to take part in "Buy Nothing Day", a day of protest against consumerism observed worldwide.

Shopping Online

Nowadays more and more people shop online. We buy all kinds of goods like clothes, shoes, electronics, fruits, and foods online. It's convenient—we just need to use a computer or cell phone to place an order and the goods will be delivered to our houses within a day or two. Another advantage is cheaper prices; usually you can save about 10% of what you pay in physical stores.

Although online shopping is common, easy and convenient, we need to watch out for its problems. The risk of identity-theft has been a serious concern, and receiving counterfeits or shoddy merchandise has also become a public outcry and outrage. However, besides these outright problems, there are also legal tricks that reputable merchants are known to play in cyberspace, and we want to guard against them, too. Online retailers may treat consumers with no-return policies by charging us for shipping costs or restocking fees for returned goods.

Part Two　Dialogue Samples

Practice the following dialogues with your partner. Change the role when necessary.

Shop Assistant: Is there anything I can do for you?

Customer: I'm trying to choose gifts. I have been here for 3 days and I am so impressed by the unique scenery of this city. Now I want to take some souvenirs for my friend.

Shop Assistant: Do you have anything particular in mind?

Customer: No, this city is still not very familiar to me, so I don't know what specialties it has, but I'd like to get something special. Would you like to give me some recommendations?

Shop Assistant: Well, there are a lot of handcrafts in our store. Let me show you some that are widely accepted by tourists from different places. I think all the handcrafts on your left hand are good options for you.

Customer: They're quite nice. But I'm afraid they're a bit expensive.

Shop Assistant: So how much are you planning to spend?

Customer: No more than three hundred yuan.

Shop Assistant: Oh, in that case, this one is OK. It is a traditional Chinese stone lion. Lion symbolizes auspice, power and stateliness in China, which can provide protection against evil spirits.

Customer: It sounds good. I think that's just what I need. Let me take a closer look at the stone lion. Oh! It looks so vivid and delicate.

Shop Assistant: Lion handcraft like this represents our traditional culture and is very popular to be sent as a gift for friend.

Customer: Oh! It's perfect. I think I'll take it. Could you wrap it, please?

Shop Assistant: OK. Wait for a moment, please.
Customer: Thank you so much.

Shop Assistant: Can I help you, sir?
Customer: Yes, I want to buy some grapes. There are so many grapes on your stall; I am wondering what kind of grape is the sweetest.

Shop Assistant: You mean you want to buy the sweetest?
Customer: I heard that grapes planted in this region are much sweeter than those from other provinces. Please give me 2 kilograms of grapes produced locally.

Shop Assistant: OK, wait a moment, please. Let me make a careful selection for you.
Customer: Make sure they are fresh.

Shop Assistant: Trust me. This bunch of grapes is not only fresh, but also sweet. I'm sure it tastes good. What else do you want?
Customer: No, thank you.

Shop Assistant: Would you pay in cash or by WeChat?
Customer: WeChat, I don't think I take enough banknotes on me.

Shop Assistant: OK. No problem.
Customer: Is a shopping bag available?

Shop Assistant: Yes, here you are! It's free!
Customer: Thank you!

Shop Assistant: Welcome to my store! Can I help you?

Customer: I am going to come back to my country and my Chinese colleagues told me that Chinese tea is famous all over the world, so I want to buy several boxes of tea for my friends.

Shop Assistant: There are various kinds of tea in our store, and some of them are very famous. Each kind of tea has its own taste. So, which kind of tea do you want?

Customer: Well, I don't know much about Chinese tea. Can you give me an introduction to all your teas?

Shop Assistant: No problem. Tea-drinking is a constituent part of Chinese culture, and we have a long history of planting tea. Here you can see are Huangshan Maofeng Tea, Biluochun Tea, Tieguanyin tea, Dahongpao tea, and Pu'er Tea. All of them are famous in China. This is green tea, and you can drink it in summer. It can relieve summer-heat and is good for your lung.

Customer: Sounds interesting. I think I have learned a lot from your introduction. The knowledge about Chinese tea is so profound that I need spend more time to understand it completely. What about this?

Shop Assistant: It is black tea and has a strong taste. It can promote digestion. The representative of black tea is Pu'er, which is from Yunnan Province. Unlike other types of tea, which are consumed not long after harvest, Pu'er tastes better with age.

Customer: Oh, I see. And what's this? It smells fragrant.

Shop Assistant: It is jasmine tea of high quality. It is fragrant and has a pleasant taste.

Customer: I will take the jasmine tea. Could you pack it with the wrapping paper and ribbon? It is a gift for my friend.

Shop Assistant: No problem. Wait for a moment.

Part Three　Useful Expressions

Expressions below may help you talk about shopping.

- shop/sales assistant 售货员
- amusement park/fun fair 游乐园/游乐场
- antique shop 古董商店
- bakery shop 面包店；糕点店
- bar/lounge bar 酒吧；休闲式高级酒吧
- barber shop 理发店
- bargain 便宜货；讲价
- book and stationery shop 书籍文具店
- butcher's shop 肉店
- cable 电话线；网线
- cash 现金
- charity shop 慈善商店
- cinema 电影院
- complaint 投诉
- convenience shop 便利店
- counter 柜台
- coupon 优惠券
- digital shop 数码商店
- discount 打折
- drinks shop 酒品专卖店
- exchange 货物调换
- gift shop 礼品店
- grocery store 食品杂货店

- invoice 发票
- laptop 笔记本电脑
- music shop 唱片行
- occupied （厕所）有人
- open market 露天市场
- outlet 廉价经销店；专营店
- parking 停车场
- perfume 香水
- pharmacy 药房
- post office 邮局
- receipt 收据
- recreation center/ground 娱乐中心/游乐场
- restaurant 餐厅，饭店
- return/refund 退货
- shopping mall 购物广场
- souvenir shop 纪念品商店
- sports shop 体育运动商店
- supermarket 超市
- supervisor 领班
- take away shop 外卖食品商店
- tax free shop 免税商店
- theatre 剧院
- till 收银机
- toy shop 玩具店
- vacant （厕所）无人
- voucher 购物券

- Can I help you?/What can I do for you?
  您想买什么?

- What size (color/kind...) do you want?
  您想买哪种型号(颜色/种类……)?

- Is this (Are these) all right?
  这个(这些)可以吗?

- What else would you like?
  您还想要什么?

- How will you pay for this?
  您用什么方式付款?

- Would you like to pay by cash or card?
  您用现金还是刷卡?

- I'm just looking, thank you.
  我只是随便看看,谢谢。

- I'm looking for...
  我想买……

- Can you show me...?
  您能给我看看……吗?

- May I take a look at it?
  看看那件可以吗?

- May I try it on?
  可以试穿吗?

- Where is the fitting room?
  试衣间在哪里?

- What is this made of?
  这是用什么做的?

- How much is it (are they)?
  多少钱?

- How much are they in all?
  一共多少钱?

- Can you come down a little?
  能便宜一点吗?

- What a steal!
  太划算了!

- Do you have this in stock?
  这个有新的吗?

- I'll take it.
  我要这件。

- Can you give me the invoice?
  您能给我发票吗?

Section B   Local Specialties

Look at the following pictures and get to know what they are about according to the describing words.

Strawberry is a kind of delicious and juicy fruit. It is one of the characteristic fruits in Panzhihua. Strawberry is rich in vitamin C and other nutrients and is good to our health. Zhongba Township (中坝乡), located in Renhe District of Panzhihua, is the main strawberry producing area. Strawberries in Panzhihua ripen from mid-November to April next year.

Navel orange is another characteristic fruit in Panzhihua. Hongge Town (红格镇) in Yanbian County of Panzhihua is the main producing area of navel orange. The orange produced here tastes sweet and is rich in vitamins. Adequate sunshine, proper temperature difference, and fertile land make oranges big and juicy, fleshy and rich in aroma.

Datian Town (大田镇), a small town in Renhe District, is 35 kilometers away from the downtown. Datian Town is famous for pomegranates. This delicious fruit is almost planted by all the households and has become the main source of income for farmers in this region. Soft-seeded pomegranate, the most famous among all the pomegranates, is rich in nutrient elements, such as amino acids, phosphorus, zinc, carbohydrates, vitamin C and vitamin B.

In Guosheng Township (国胜乡) of Yanbian County, there stands Bailing Mountain, the highest mountain in Panzhihua City. The town is famous for Guosheng tea. Guosheng tea belongs to green tea and is rich in 11 minerals such as potassium, calcium, magnesium and manganese. It is not only a precious natural drink, but also helps to keep beauty and health.

5

Mango, a kind of tropical fruit, is one of the specialties of Panzhihua. Mangoes here are rich in variety and have a mellow taste. If you like mango, welcome to Panzhihua. Here, you can eat mango all year round. Adequate sunshine and suitable temperature provide unique environmental conditions for the growth of mango. If you want to bring your friends some fruits from Panzhihua, mango can be your best choice.

6

Loquat is one of the most popular fruits during the Spring Festival in southern regions of China. Miyi County and Yanbian County in Panzhihua are the main producing areas of loquat. Loquat here is famous for its big size, thick fruit flesh, thin skin and rich flavor. Loquat is also an traditional Chinese medicine, which can be used to treat cough.

7

Cherry is a fruit rich in vitamins and one of the characteristic fruits in Panzhihua as well. Wuben Township (务本乡), Pingdi Town (平地镇) and Zhongba Township in Miyi County are the main cherry planting areas. However, cherry produced in Huangcao Township (黄草乡) is the best because of its unique light and heat conditions. Huangcao Township is about 80 kilometers away from Panzhihua City. If you like cherries, welcome to Miyi to taste the biggest and sweetest cherries.

8

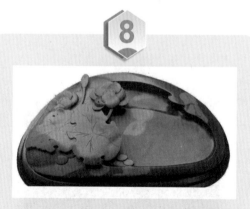

As we all know, inkstone is one of the four treasures of ancient Chinese study. Juque inkstone (苴却砚) is a kind of famous inkstone in China, and also an important specialty of Panzhihua. Juque inkstone is made from the unique stone in Panzhihua—Juque stone. The inkstone is mainly manufactured in Renhe District of Panzhihua City. It has rich patterns, gorgeous colors and excellent quality, and is loved by men of literature and writing.

 ## Section C   Oral Practices

Part One   Describing Pictures

Look at the following pictures and talk with your partner using the prompting words.

01 Termite Mushroom Oil

Prompting words: specialty; termite mushroom; flavor; fragrance

02 Jianchang Dried Salted Duck

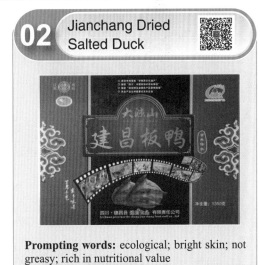

Prompting words: ecological; bright skin; not greasy; rich in nutritional value

03 Yanyuan Apple

Prompting words: Yanyuan County; high altitude; semi-drought climate; abundant sunshine; crispy; juicy

04 Sichuan Sausage

Prompting words: traditional food; sweet and spicy tastes; casing; delicious

05 Grape Wine

Prompting words: grape; rich in nutrition; high-quality; wine-brewing technology

06 Buckwheat Tea

Prompting words: buckwheat seeds; golden yellow; good to health; lingering fragrance

07 Truffle

Prompting words: rare and expensive; fragrant; marbling; nutritious

08 Lacquer Ware of the Yi Nationality

Prompting words: tableware; folk handcraft; tourist souvenir

Part Two Group Discussion

Discuss the following topics with your partner.

1. **Talk about online shopping.**

   What are the advantages and disadvantages of online shopping?

   How to shop online?

   Can you describe one of your experiences of shopping online?

2. **Talk about rational shopping.**

   What's the meaning of rational shopping?

   How to shop rationally?

   What are the results of irrational shopping?

3. **Talk about how to bargain.**

   Do you always bargain when shopping?

   Describe your own bargain tricks.

4. **Talk about new ways of payment.**

   List some new ways of payment.

   What are the advantages and disadvantages of these new ways of payment?

5. **Talk about brand and after-sale.**

   Will you take after-sale into consideration when shopping?

   Brand or after-sale, which one is more important? Why?

Section D   Extended Reading

Read the following passage that may help you better understand the topic of this unit.

Chinese Firm Behind the "Amazon Coat" Hits Jackpot in the US

A $129.99 winter coat by Chinese fashion label Orolay has become a number one best-seller on Amazon, becoming so popular it is now known as the "Amazon coat", after going viral on social media.

The Women's Thickened Down Jacket has been reviewed more than 6,000 times on the e-commerce site and comes in five colors, with shoppers saying they are delighted to have got their hands on one. Its success is due in part to the influence of shoppers' peers, according to Alexis DeSalva, a senior retail and e-commerce analyst at consultancy Mintel. 56% of women aged 18 to 34 would be willing to buy something because a friend posted about it on social media, compared to 38% for all age-groups, according to a survey. Some shoppers will be attracted by the element of discovery, according to Michelle Whelan, Chief Executive of Marketing Agency Geometry UK. "Influencers, celebrities, moms and teens are all connected through the purchase of a coat. An unknown coat (not a Canada Goose expensive coat) available on the most democratic retail platform in the world, at a price that everyone can afford." Whelan said.

The viral jacket is made by a Chinese company called Orolay and its jackets contain 90% duck-down filling, which is the same amount you'd find in Canada Goose's $800 parkas. Business Insider suggested that the affordable cost of the viral down parka by Orolay should terrify Canada Goose. Buyers comment: "I love this jacket. Got it at XS and it fit perfectly—no tightness, no wind getting from under the jacket and no fabric stretching!" "I like the pockets, which can store my phone, purse, gloves, camera and every other necessity for an outdoor trip." "It's super warm. I wore it with only a T-shirt and leggings and went outdoors when there was moderate snow and temperature was -3 degrees Celsius or 27 degrees Fahrenheit outdoors. The surface is water-resistant and the snow glides away on the surface."

The founder of Orolay Kevin Qiu did not expect such success. When he left his job in 2012 to try his luck at starting an online apparel business in a rural Chinese city, his main goal was to carve out more time to spend with his wife and newborn child. It never entered his mind that his Orolay puffer jacket would become a huge hit, celebrated as the "Amazon Coat" in the US social and traditional media—and held up as a budding rival to premium brand Canada Goose.

Using duck down sourced from China's Hebei and Anhui provinces, the polyester coats are priced between $80 and $139. By contrast, Canada Goose jackets start from about $575 in the United States. Orolay's success is, however, not just a tale of competitive pricing and a design that found favor with US consumers.

Qiu is among a wave of Chinese merchants that have benefited from new measures introduced by Amazon in recent years that have made it easy for overseas vendors to sell on its site.

Analysts say the number of Chinese merchants selling on Amazon's US site began to pick up over the last five years after it introduced measures that allowed sellers worldwide to store products at Amazon warehouses and provided help shipping those goods to customers.

Qiu credits Amazon for much of the firm's success but is thinking of branching out. Expansion plans include extending Orolay's product line to cotton clothing and men's outerwear. But for now, Qiu is still marveling at how his business has become so successful in a market he barely knows.

国产羽绒服登顶美国亚马逊

近日，中国时尚品牌欧绒莱生产的一款售价 129.99 美元的冬装外套成为亚马逊的头号爆款，此前这款外套走红社交网络，如今由于太受欢迎，被人们称为"亚马逊外套"。

这款女士加厚羽绒服有五种颜色，在亚马逊上已被评论超过 6 000 次，买家纷纷表示他们很高兴买到这款羽绒服。咨询公司 Mintel 的高级零售和电商分析师亚历克西斯·迪萨瓦表示，这款产品的成功在一定程度上归功于买家群体效应。调查显示，年龄在 18~34 岁之间的女性中，56% 的人会因为朋友在社交媒体上发布了某样东西，而愿意购买同样的东西。相较而言，在全年龄组中，这一比例为 38%。英国市场营销机构 Geometry 首席执行官米歇尔·惠兰表示，一些购物者会被发现元素所吸引。"网红、名人、母亲和青

少年通过购买一件外套被联系在一起。一款不知名的外套（不像加拿大鹅那么贵），在全球最大众化的零售平台上可以买到，而且价格人人付得起。"惠兰说。

这款风靡全美的夹克是一家名为欧绒莱（Orolay）的中国公司生产的，夹克中90%的填充物都是鸭绒，这和加拿大鹅售价800美元的派克大衣的填充物含量是一样的。商业内幕网认为，欧绒莱公司的爆款羽绒服价格实惠，对加拿大鹅构成威胁。买家评论道："我特别喜欢这件大衣，我买的是XS码，非常合身——不勒身、不透风，布料也很结实！""我喜欢衣服上的口袋，可以放手机、钱包、手套、相机和其他出门必需品。""这件衣服超级暖和。我里面只穿一件T恤和一条打底裤，就能在下着中雪、室外气温零下3摄氏度或27华氏度的时候出门。衣服表面是防水的，雪会从衣服上滑下来。"

欧绒莱公司的创始人邱佳伟并没预想到这一成功。邱佳伟先生在2012年辞了职，打算在一个小城市开一家服装网店碰碰运气。当时他的主要目的是多留出时间陪陪妻子和刚出生的宝宝。邱先生没想到，自己的羽绒服品牌欧绒莱会成为一大热门，在美国社交媒体和传统纸媒上被誉为"亚马逊外套"，并且被推举为加拿大鹅这一高端品牌的新晋竞争对手。

这种涤纶面料的羽绒服，选用的是产自中国河北省和安徽省的鸭绒，价格在80至139美元之间。相比之下，加拿大鹅的羽绒服在美国售价是575美元起。然而，欧绒莱成功故事的背后，不只是颇具竞争力的价格和备受美国消费者青睐的设计。

近年来，亚马逊推出新举措，海外卖家在亚马逊上架销售更方便了。一大批中国商人受益于此，邱先生也是其中之一。

分析人员称，在过去五年中，开始有越来越多的中国商户入驻美国亚马逊商城，原因在于该网站推出的新举措：允许全球卖家在亚马逊的库房内存放货品，并且还提供送货服务，将这些商品送到顾客手上。

邱先生认为，公司能够如此成功，多亏亚马逊商城；不过他正考虑拓展业务。扩展计划包括将欧绒莱的产品线扩展到棉质服装和男式外套。但在当下，邱先生还是觉得很惊讶：自己的业务居然能在自己并不太了解的美国市场如此风靡！

Unit 6
Sports & Health

Objectives

1. To know useful information about sports and health
2. To practice dialogues about doing exercises
3. To describe pictures about sports and health
4. To discuss topics about sports and health

Warm-up Questions

① Do you like sports? What's your favorite sport?
② What kinds of sports are popular in China?
③ What are the advantages and disadvantages of playing outdoor sports?

Section A   Getting Ready to Speak

Part One   Reading for Information

Read the following passages and get useful information about sports and health.

Sports and Healthy Body

A healthy body is necessary for a healthy mind. As is known, to have a sound mind, we must have a sound body first. This is of vital importance. Only by keeping ourselves healthy and strong can we be energetic and vigorous in studying and working and live a happy life.

To keep ourselves fit, physical exercise is the best way. Taking part in outdoor sports, we are closer to nature and can take in fresh air. The beauty of nature will keep us clear-headed, which is essential to our health. Besides, sports stimulate circulation of blood and help to excrete wastes in the body. Sports can also stimulate our appetite and activate our digestion. As a result, we can become strong-bodied.

People taking an active part in physical exercises will enjoy good health. They seldom get sick and feel vigorous even when working for a whole day. So keep up doing physical exercises, live longer and do more for our country.

Benefits of Physical Activity

For thousands of years, physical activity has been associated with health. Today, science has confirmed the link, with overwhelming evidence that people who lead active lifestyles are less likely to die early, or to experience major illnesses such as heart disease, diabetes and colon cancer.

Exercise benefits every part of the body, including the mind. Exercising stimulates the body to produce endorphins, chemicals that lead a person to feel peaceful and happy. Exercise can help people sleep better. It can also help with mental health issues such as mild depression and self-esteem. Plus, exercise can give people a real sense of accomplishment and pride at having achieved a certain goal—like beating an old time in the 100-meter dash.

Exercising can help you look better, too. People who exercise burn calories and look in better shape than those who don't. In fact, exercise is one of the most important ways of keeping your body at a healthy weight. When you exercise, you burn food calories for fuel. If a person eats more calories than he or she burns, the body stores them away as fat. Exercise can help burn these stored calories.

Finally, exercising to maintain a healthy weight also decreases a person's risk of developing certain diseases, including type II diabetes and high blood pressure.

Cycling

Along with jogging and swimming, cycling is one of the best all-round forms of exercises. It can help to increase your strength and energy. But increasing your strength is not the only advantage of cycling. When cycling, you're not carrying the weight of your body on your feet, so it's a good form of exercise for people with painful feet or backs. However, for all forms of exercises it's important to start slowly and build up gently. Doing too much or too quickly can damage muscles that aren't used to working. Ideally you should cycle at least two or three times a week. It can work better if you get a little out of breath when cycling. Don't worry if you begin to lose your breath. Shortness of breath shows that the exercise is having the right effect. However, if you feel in pain then you should stop and take a rest.

Part Two   Dialogue Samples

Practice the following dialogues with your partner. Change the role when necessary.

Jane: Hello, my name is Jane and I'd like to ask a few questions about getting fit.

Instructor: Hi, Jane. What can I do for you?

Jane: I need to get in shape.

Instructor: Well, you've come to the right place. Have you been doing any exercise lately?

Jane: I'm afraid not.

Instructor: OK. We'll start off slowly. Which type of exercise do you enjoy doing?

Jane: I like doing aerobics, but I hate jogging. I don't mind doing some weight-lifting.

Instructor: Great! How often can you work out?

Jane: Twice or three times a week would be good.

Instructor: Why don't we start with an aerobics class twice a week followed by a little weight lifting?

Jane: Sounds fine to me.

Instructor: You need to start slowly and build up gradually to three or four times a week.

Jane: OK. What equipment should I prepare?

Instructor: You need to prepare a leotard and some sneakers.

Jane: Is that all? How do I sign up for the classes?

Instructor: You need to join the gym and then choose the classes that fit your schedule best.

Jane: Great! I can't wait to get started. Thanks for your advice.

Instructor: You're welcome. I'll see you in aerobics class!

Todd: Mike, I know you're good at strength training. Would you give me some advice about how to train the lower body and legs? I actually don't want to lift weights with my legs. Is it OK if I just skip it?

Mike: Well, you should train your legs because a full body workout is very important.

Todd: OK, so what exercises should I do?

Mike: I think you should start off squatting. Make sure you have a squat rack, and then put the bar behind your head on your shoulders and you just squat as if you are sitting on a bench and come back up.

Todd: When do the squat, how low should I go? Should I go until I'm almost sitting on the floor?

Mike: Just as there is a bench underneath your bottom. And basically, your legs and your knees should be about 90 degrees.

Todd: OK. Will it exercise all my legs?

Mike: No. It mainly exercises your hamstrings and bottom.

Todd: No calves? Then what should I do for my calves?

Mike: You can do calf raises on a squat rack. Hold the bar in the same position as you do a squat and raise your legs up on your toes.

Todd: How many should I do?

Mike: I think ten times for three sets is appropriate for a beginner.

Todd: OK, I remember. Thanks a lot, Mike. I'm gonna get started.

Mike: You're welcome and fighting!

Lilei: I don't understand why you always look so happy, so energetic. It seems like you've got good news every day.

Eric: Really? Do I look happy all the time?

Lilei: Yes!

Eric: I would owe it to my habit of doing exercises. I feel alive after exercising!

Lilei: Oh, I know. I saw you doing pull-ups one time on the playground and some students trying to imitate you.

Eric: Yeah, they are doing it for fun. Few people want to do exercises like me. It's difficult and boring.

Lilei: It's true. Many students do exercises when they have to. We have PE once a week.

Eric: But I think Chinese students need to exercise more. And exercise will help them learn new things better.

Lilei: And it can make bodies stronger. I should take some exercise then. Do you have any suggestions?

Eric: Well, do what you like to do. It can be anything. Jogging, cycling, playing ping-pong, playing basketball, and so on. Exercising for three or four times a week is appropriate. But remember to do some stretches first.

Lilei: Oh, I know. Thank you.

Eric: Not at all.

Part Three   Useful Expressions

Expressions below may help you talk about sports and health.

- allergy 过敏
- all-round champion 全能冠军
- anxiety 焦虑
- bad temper 坏脾气；暴躁
- balanced diet 均衡饮食
- ball games 球类运动
- champion/gold medalist 冠军
- cheer-leader 啦啦队长
- coach 教练
- cold 流感
- cough 咳嗽
- depression 抑郁
- energetic 精力旺盛的
- faint 昏厥
- fever 发烧
- first aid 急救
- good living habits 良好的生活习惯
- health 健康；身体状况；卫生
- heart attack 心脏病发作
- high jump 跳高
- hockey 曲棍球
- in good/bad health 身体好/差
- injection 注射
- lack of appetite 食欲不振

- long jump 跳远
- medical examination 体检
- near-sighted/short-sighted 近视的
- neglect of exercise 缺乏运动
- obesity 肥胖
- over fatigue 过度疲劳
- overload 负担过重
- painkiller 止痛药
- physical disorder 身体不适
- physical exercise therapy/sports therapy 体育疗法
- physical training 体育锻炼
- referee 裁判员
- relay race 接力
- running nose 流鼻涕
- second/silver medalist 亚军
- sleep disorder 睡眠失常
- spectator 观众
- sports fan/enthusiast 运动爱好者
- sports/sporting activity 体育活动
- stress 压力
- sub-health 亚健康
- team event 团体项目
- test 检查
- third/bronze medalist 第三名
- vomit 呕吐
- world-record holder 世界纪录保持者

- Good health is above wealth.
  健康胜于财富。

- An apple a day keeps the doctor away.
  一天一苹果，医生远离我。

- A close mouth catches no ies.
  病从口入。

- An ounce of prevention is worth a ponce of cure.
  预防为主，治疗为辅。

- Wealth is nothing without health.
  没有健康，钱再多也没用。

- Regular physical exercises can strengthen one's resistance against illness.
  经常锻炼身体能够提高人体的免疫力。

- The most important thing in the Olympic Games is not to win but to participate.
  奥林匹克运动会重在参与，而不是取胜。

- The most important thing in the Games is not the triumph but the struggle; not to have conquered but to have fought well.
  比赛中最重要的不是胜利，而是奋斗；不是征服，而是奋力拼搏。

- Sloth, like rust, consumes faster than labor wears.
  懒惰像生锈一样，比操劳更能消耗身体。

- He keeps exercising all year around, even in the hottest days in summer and the coldest days in winter.

他常年坚持锻炼，冬练三九，夏练三伏。

- She is very busy at work, but she manages to stick to her exercise regime.
  虽然工作很忙，但是她还坚持锻炼。

- She fixes the exercise time for Saturday afternoons.
  她把锻炼的时间固定在星期六下午。

- Doing sit-ups is an effective way to exercise abdominal muscles.
  仰卧起坐是锻炼腹部肌肉的有效方法。

- Thanks to his persistent physical exercise, he looks healthy, with white hair and a ruddy complexion.
  因为长期坚持体育锻炼，他看起来鹤发童颜。

- A sound mind dwells in a sound body.
  健全的精神寓于健康的身体。

- Early to bed and early to rise makes a man healthy.
  早睡早起身体好。

- Prevention is better than cure.
  预防胜于治疗。

- Reading is to the mind while exercise to the body.
  读书健脑，运动强身。

- The first wealth is health.
  健康是人生第一财富。

- A light heart lives long.
  豁达者长寿。

Section B   Local Specialties

Look at the following pictures and get to know what they are about according to the describing words.

1

Hiking is kind of long and vigorous walk, usually on trails in the countryside. Studies suggest that hiking has great health benefits, such as keeping fit and releasing stress. Hiking is also a good chance to get close to nature.

2

On Dec. 9, 2018, about 110 riders from 18 international professional teams participated in Tour Panzhihua International Road Cycling Race. The race started from the Third-Front Construction Museum. Along the Yalong River and the Jinsha River, the track passed through Ertan National Forest Park and Ertan Dam, and ended at Miyi Cultural Square. The whole journey was 114.7 kilometers long.

3

Rock climbing is a sport in which participants climb up, down or across natural rock formations or artificial rock walls. The goal is to reach the summit of a formation or the endpoint of a usually pre-defined route without falling. When climb rocks, you need to use all your muscles, so it can strength your body and make you stronger.

4

Archery, different from what people usually think, is not necessarily a highly professional sport in the Olympic Games. In real life, it is also a leisure sport with no age limitation and low threshold. Engaging in archery scientifically can not only strengthen arms, chest, waist and legs, exercise muscles and eyesight, and improve physical fitness, but also improve their respiratory endurance, make the body more flexible, and make people more focused, and respond to the outside world faster and more accurately.

Rafting and whitewater rafting are recreational outdoor activities which use an inflatable raft to cross a river. This is often done on whitewater or different levels of rough water. Such sports need the ability of dealing with risk and teamwork.

Aerobic exercise refers to physical exercise conducted by human body under the condition of adequate supply of oxygen. In simple terms, aerobic exercise is a kind of low-intensity, rhythmic exercise with a longer duration (about 30 minutes or more).

Basketball is a team sport in which two teams, most commonly of five players each, competing with one another on a rectangular court. Their goal is to shoot a basketball through the opposing team's hoop while preventing the opposing team from shooting through their own hoop. There are various forms of basketball games, such as the common five-a-side basketball game and the popular street three-a-side basketball game.

Martial arts or Wushu, are traditional Chinese sports that pay equal attention to inner and outer practice. It can defend enemy attack and can also strengthen the body. Martial arts are not only able to develop one's bravery and fortitude, but are also good ways to promote self-cultivation. "Never learn skills before learning courtesy, never learn martial arts before learning their morals." By learning martial arts and their morals, you will respect teachers and confirm with social norms, and will grow into reasonable, trustworthy, righteous and courageous men that will never bully others.

 ## Section C   Oral Practices

Part One   Describing Pictures

Look at the following pictures and talk with your partner using the prompting words.

01 Healthy Lifestyle

Prompting words: Zhuhu Park; sing; dance; practice Taichi; climb mountains

02 Outdoor Activities

Prompting words: hiking; jogging; cycling; rock climbing; camping; flying kites

03 Watching the Seagulls

Prompting words: fresh air; feed; seagull; relaxing; harmonious

04 Football

Prompting words: football clubs; teenagers; work out; energetic

05 Health Care

Prompting words: health resort; nursing homes; livable environment; pleasant temperature; proper humidity

06 Cycling

Prompting words: aerobic exercise; low-impact; protect from diseases

07 Citywide Sports Meeting

Prompting words: nationwide fitness; competitive; spirit of sports

08 Outdoor Orienteering

Prompting words: orienteering; endurance; sense of direction; cross-country

Part Two   Group Discussion

Discuss the following topics with your partner.

1. **Talk about the saying "Life is movement.".**

    What is the relationship between sports and health?

    What are the advantages of doing sports?

    How is doing sports good for health?

2. **Talk about your favorite sport.**

    What is your favorite sport?

    Why do you like it best?

    How often do you exercise?

3. **Talk about ways to keep healthy.**

    How is your health condition?

    In your daily life, how do you keep healthy?

    What are you going to do to keep healthy?

4. **Talk about the saying "Health is above the wealth.".**

    Do you agree with the saying "Health is above the wealth."? Why or why not?

    What is the relationship between health and wealth?

5. **Talk about the saying "He is wise that knows when he is well enough.".**

    What's your opinion on the saying "He is wise that knows when he is well enough."?

    Are you content with your life?

    How to balance the relationship between contentment and ambition?

Section D   Extended Reading

Read the following passage that may help you better understand the topic of this unit.

Walking and Health

Most of us will admit we could probably do with getting a bit fitter. Joining the gym, exercise classes and personal trainers can be really expensive, and realistically most of us have to spend our cash elsewhere. But that isn't a good enough excuse not to do anything, and there's one form of exercise which is completely free—walking.

It's a great way to explore new areas, and it can also be the perfect opportunity for a proper chat with your nearest and dearest away from screens and everyday stresses. And there are also lots of health benefits to walking. Back in 2013, an NHS study revealed more walking could save 37,000 lives in England every single year.

Walking is astonishingly powerful and scientifically proven by study after study—walking transforms your body and mind. In fact, research shows it can add almost two years to your life. Of course, there's the major perk that sneaking in those steps helps you shed unwanted weight; one Canadian study found that an hour-long brisk walk every day reduced belly fat in women by 20% over 14 weeks. But going for a trek can benefit your body in other significant ways, too. Here's how:

It guards your brain. Two hours of walking per week cuts your risk of stroke by 30%. Hitting the road also protects brain regions associated with planning and memory, and doing it for 30 minutes a day has even been found to reduce symptoms of depression by 36%.

It strengthens your bones. Four hours of walking per week can slash your chances of a hip fracture by up to 43%. In other words, the more you move now, the more mobile you'll be later in life.

It improves your heart health. Take a stroll for your ticker: A new study of more than 89,000 women found that those who walked briskly for 40 minutes two or three times per week had up to a 38% lower chance of heart failure after menopause than those who did it less often or more slowly. What's more, researchers have found that walking for just 20 minutes per day lowers your risk of heart disease by 30%, and it can also cut your risk of obesity (a major risk factor for heart disease) in half.

Though she has tried everything from kettlebells to Gyrokinesis, personal trainer and fitness video guru Jessica Smith says walking remains her workout of choice for fitness and weight control. "I truly believe it's the best way to get and stay in shape," she says. "Not only is it free, anyone can do it and you don't need any equipment to begin. It's easy on the joints, and I believe it helps with appetite control."—unlike with running, she feels less hungry after walking, not more.

步行和健康

大多数人都想更健康一点。去健身房、上健身课、请私人教练可能要支付昂贵的费用，但现实是，绝大多数人都会把钱花在其他地方。但这并不是不做事的借口，因为有一种锻炼是不花钱的——散步！

这是探索新环境的极佳方式，也是远离屏幕和日常压力、与最亲近的人好好聊聊的绝佳机会。此外，散步对健康也有很多好处。早在 2013 年，英国国民健康体系的研究就已揭示：多走路可每年拯救 37 000 位英国人的生命。

步行是非常有用的，一项项科学研究证明——步行能改变你的身心。事实上，研究表明，步行可以将你的生命延长近两年。当然，在步行中还有额外收获，那就是能帮助你减掉身上的赘肉；加拿大的一项研究发现，每天快走一小时，女性可在 14 周内减掉 20% 的腹部脂肪。不过，徒步行走也可以在其他方面对你的身体有所裨益。下面是几大好处：

它能保护大脑。每周步行两小时可将中风风险降低 30%。走路还能保护和计划、记忆相关的大脑区域。而且，研究甚至发现每天步行 30 分钟能将抑郁症的症状减轻 36%。

它能强化骨骼。每周步行四小时可以使髋部骨折概率降低43%。换句话说，你现在动得越多，你晚年生活行动就越方便。

它能促进心脏健康。为了你的心脏，多散散步吧：一项针对超过89 000名女性的新研究发现，那些每周进行两到三次40分钟快走的人，绝经后的心脏衰竭概率比那些快走次数少或慢的人低38%。更重要的是，研究人员发现，每天步行20分钟就能降低30%的心脏病风险，同时还可以降低一半的肥胖风险，而肥胖是心脏病的主要危险因素。

虽然私人教练兼健身视频专家杰西卡·史密斯尝试了从壶铃到回旋运动的所有锻炼方式，但她说步行仍然是她健身和控制体重的首选。"我真的认为这是获得并保持好体形的最好方法。"她说，"它不仅是免费的，而且任何人都可以做，你不需要任何设备就可以开始。它对关节很友好，而且我认为它有助于控制食欲。"这一点和跑步不同，她在步行后感觉不那么饿，而跑步后则会觉得更饿。